From Suffering to Healing

When your Heart Breaks. When your Soul is Longing. You need Answers. You need Healing.

Trinity Royal

SK Royals LLC

Library of Congress Control Number: 2022901725

Digital - ISBN: 978-1-957681-05-4

Paperback – ISBN: 978-1-957681-06-1

Free Gift to our Readers

Metamorphosis

From Darkness to Light

https://mailchi.mp/d2ec904366cb/metamorphosis-freeg-ift

 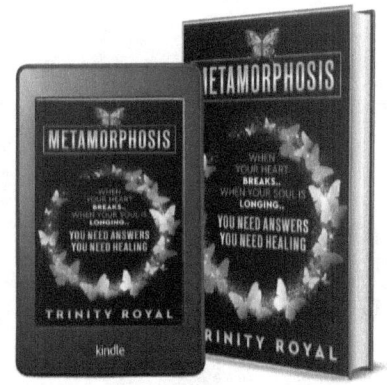

Introduction

I am a forest, and a night of dark trees: but
he who is not afraid of my darkness, will
find banks full of roses under my cypresses.
– Friedrich Nietzsche

———— ··•·· ————

Life is made up of moments. Every moment is a point in
time to make a choice. The series of choices that you make
as you progress become your life's journey. The physical
body that you currently inhabit also happens to be the
vessel that embodies your soul. The soul is the deepest and
most complete expression of a person. Some authors will
use the word 'soul' almost interchangeably with 'spirit' or
even liken it to the mind. Herein, mostly the soul is spoken
about more than the mind or spirit. Your real and true

identity is your soul. Every soul that has ever existed in its creation is unique and identifiable by its soul signature which is as distinctive as a fingerprint.

The purpose of your soul's existence is to have experiences and to grow into its fullest expression. As you grow through different stages of life, you are influenced by your surroundings including the people and places you come into contact with.

When you were born, your family impressed a name upon you as an infant. Consciously or subconsciously, what your family believed and the notions of acceptable and unacceptable were also imprinted upon you without your input or consent. Then, as you grew into childhood, the education system that you entered into further influenced your experience and existence. In high school, the adolescent version of you may have sought the acceptance of your peers or other people in your community, and their values were then fixed upon you. These things became internalized in you as you either accepted or rejected these ideals. The same process happens at work when you are playing your professional role, or at home when you are in your familial role. Everywhere, your soul is inundated with the energy of others.

Power is constantly flowing throughout the universe, and the soul is bathed in this constant flow of energy. What you choose to do with the energy determines your soul's experiences. Some of your experiences contribute to your soul's growth and development, while other experiences might not. The soul is meant to experience a multitude of trials and tribulations along its journey. You might wonder where your soul is journeying to, and the answer is that your soul is on a quest to enrich itself and then return back to its source of origin in the universe. The universe is structured to assist your soul in making choices. In a way, the universe is in a conspiracy for your soul's growth as it is in the world's favor for you to grow fully into your soul's potential.

During this journey, your soul has acquired—and will continue to acquire—various experiences, both good and bad, favorable and unfavorable, positive and negative. However, to continue its journey back to the source of its creation, all of the residual bad, unfavorable, negative energy has to be discarded. When you shed that negative residue, your energetic vibration will be high enough for your soul to endure the frequencies of the higher realms.

The Buddha said, "All I teach is suffering and the end of suffering." He also mentioned "The root of all suffering is attachment". Suffering in his teaching does not necessarily mean grave physical pain, but rather the mental suffering we undergo when our tendency to hold onto pleasure encounters the fleeting nature of life, and our experiences become unsatisfying and ungovernable. On some level we understand it, yet we resist it.

Everyone suffers. It's part of the human condition. Yet suffering can be the doorway to your personal evolution, to growth and expansion, if you choose to shift your thoughts and perceptions.

The bad news is: We are the creators of our suffering.

The good news is: We are the creators of our suffering.

This book will help facilitate your soul's journey into the higher frequencies on its way back home to source.

Chapter 1

Roadmap from A to Z

Please know that although you might be struggling now, someday you will look back and realize what you went through changed your life in many ways for the better. – Karen Salmansohn

The following chapters take you and your soul on a side journey. The goal of this experience is to move you one step closer from where you are right now to where you want to be. First, we discuss exactly what we mean when we talk about the soul and all that it entails. The idea of a soul is ancient and ubiquitous in global cultures throughout history. Once we have a thorough understanding of the soul's inherent beauty and purpose, we can examine the question of why the soul undergoes trials and tribulations in its journey. Then, we talk about the purpose of suffering and delve into the specific question of how long the suffering must last before you emerge from the darkness. Sometimes, suffering is unexplained, and you will learn about different types of karma and karmic influences that contribute to this experience.

Afterward, we will take a look at how suffering manifests in the world, in general, and in your world specifically. You will come to understand how suffering is also the key to your soul's awakening and an essential player in the evolution of your soul's metamorphosis. Both the positive and negative aspects of suffering are equally true, and there are gifts to be found in your darkness that we will illuminate.

As old as the soul is the concept of a "dark night of the soul", which is a time of great suffering that we will dissect. This book will teach you everything you need to know about the dark night of the soul. You will discover the different ways that a dark night can enter into your life's journey, and you will be able to recognize when your soul is going through one so that you may proceed in accordance with it rather than fight against it. You will know what to expect from this experience, which is a period of palpable disunion with your soul, and learn how to choose to take the road that leads to spiritual awakening. Many liken this brand of suffering to a deep depression, but we will compare the two experiences for you to understand their important differences. In both cases, your light awaits on the other side of the darkness of suffering.

Finally, we examine how to heal yourself. Each suggested method is worth books unto itself, and they're offered as tools to add to your repertoire of self-healing techniques. You will begin to know how healing happens and where to turn for more help once you believe that you can heal yourself. Healing is a lifelong learning experience that you are awakened to along your soul's journey through suffering, and this book will teach you what to do and what not to do on your self-healing journey. As you learn how to release stuck negative, emotional energy in your body, you will see that the treatment for a dark night of the soul is quite different from the treatment for depression.

By the end of this reading experience, you will be able to determine for yourself what causes suffering in you and your daily life. You will know your triggers and symptoms. You will know why suffering happens to you and what control over it you have. You will be able to answer the question of why bad things happen to good people, and you will understand why some suffering is directly related to your soul's true purpose and destiny. You will have intimate knowledge of the characteristics of suffering.

For the duration of these pages, whether you are reading to understand your personal suffering or that of another person, allow the many questions that arise to urge you forward in the spirit of curiosity. Depending on your reasons for reading this book and where you are in your soul's journey, the answers presented here will bring an awareness and greater understanding of your own life's journey.

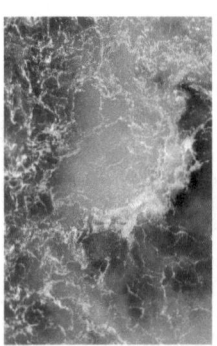

Hopefully, regardless of why you are here, you will come away with the ability to put words to an inexplicable experience. Take heart, for you are entering deep waters. Seat-belt on.

Chapter 2

Why Your Soul Journey Matters

Our wounds are often the openings into the best and most beautiful part of us. – David Richo

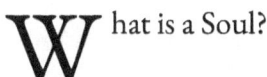

W hat is a Soul?

The Souls is the 'Divine Flame' – a metaphor used to describe the essence of Divine Life which is drawn into the individual being at the moment of conception. Therefore, the Soul is the core of your being.

You Soul is Divine Reality, Divine Intelligence, Divine Love which is powerful Divine impulse to create grow, nourish, nurture, heal, protect, fulfill every need, within a system of perfect law and order.

Why your Soul journey matters?

Because the soul is the deepest expression of a person, the soul is also the source of the greatest pain. The most extreme human suffering is not called a "dark night of the mind" or a "dark night of the spirit" but is referred to as a "dark night of the soul", which we will get into soon. This level of pain and transformation only occurs at the soul level.

The diversity of soul paths is near limitless. You can choose to specialize in any area you want. You can change course, take on multiple interests, diverge from what is expected of you at every turn and create your own narrative for how you want to progress. It's entirely within your free-will.

Once the Soul has enough experience, a desire to become perfections is born. The soul seeks union with the Whole. It is the upon the realization of this desire for God-likeness that the individual is "born again of the Spirit." The partnership of God and man has been consummated and the eternal adventure begins.

This soul journey brings you to and through deep suffering. During this time, you will come face to face with the heaviest questions that you could ever ask yourself, such as:

You cannot answer these questions until you ask them, and you will ask them when you go through darkness that ripples through your soul. This is transformation, and it is a part of your soul's journey.

The answers to these questions are not always logical. What you perceive as a curse is really a blessing, but this is an absurd answer to the question of why you're alive. To say your suffering is divinely intended is an insult—but it is also true.

It's not your fault that it doesn't make sense. For your entire life, your mind has been conditioned to believe certain things. You grew up believing that something outside of yourself would one day make you happy. Maybe you thought it was money, a beautiful spouse, a good career, or your dream house or car. When you put your happiness into something that is outside of you, you actually forfeit happiness. You lose. If happiness is something you need to pursue or something you need to attain, then it is not true happiness. Real happiness is right here, in this moment. It is inside of you. When you can't feel it, it's because it's smothered by other things that you're also holding onto inside of yourself.

If this still sounds like a ridiculous answer, then perhaps at least you feel a twinge that there is truth in it. As you peel back layer by layer to reveal your most authentic self, this truth becomes easier and easier to grasp. There is a "real you" trapped inside the darkness.

Imagine a butterfly as it begins to emerge from its cocoon. The creature must struggle to break free. The butterfly's physical struggle is what strengthens its wings. If the butterfly is forced from its cocoon prematurely, it will not be able to fly because its wings are not strong enough. The tempering stage is crucial and must be endured.

Abstractly, this same principle holds true for trees and flowers. Without the wind, trunks and stems would not be coaxed to build the structural strength that allows them to remain upright.

This applies to you, too. To change, you need to struggle. Your Soul Journey will lead you to challenges; these challenges will lead you to Metamorphosis. Very rarely does growth happen without challenges.

True, authentic spiritual growth requires immense struggle and the experience of personal tragedy. These are what grow you. When you suffer to this degree, it is not intended to be a test of your spiritual elitism. Instead, suffering simply arises from the circumstances of your life. You must detach from the idea that it is a bad thing that should not be happening. It will happen. Suffering is part of an ongoing spiritual process that helps to liberate you from the very attachments and compulsions that you suffer from. Suffering can empower you to live and love more freely, but you have to let go of old ways of thinking that are painful and occasionally devastating because they no longer serve your soul's journey.

When you suffer, your ego (which is your false self) dies a little bit each time. Ego is that part of you that needs to be liked and accepted. Ego is who you tell yourself you are or who you have been told you are. Ego is not your true self, though, and it needs to experience the death that suffering brings. To evolve on your soul's journey, you need to shed the ego because it keeps the essence of you confined to a mental construct, and this greatly impedes your growth.

Everyone is born with a soul, but not everyone will fully embrace their soul's journey and learn to incorporate their suffering into their experience during this lifetime. The majority of people live an ego-centered life rather than a soul-centered life. This means that people on the whole are unable to accurately understand another person's point of view or experience. 'Egocentrism' is observable at all stages of a person's development from infancy through adulthood. What happens at these stages is that people are more focused on the external world and other people in it, so they base their decisions and actions on what their ego perceives as favorable. Adults can appear less egocentric as they mature, but this is sometimes because they have learned to correct their perspective rather than genuinely shed their ego. Imagine, instead, a soul-centered existence that is guided by intuition, mindfulness, empathy, and inner wisdom. This kind of life is worth the suffering it takes to crack you open, drain your outdated contents, and fill you with a reimagined vision for your life and your role in the world.

Before any true growth or healing can occur—before transformation can occur—there must necessarily be a process of destruction and complete annihilation of everything false that you thought was true. Everything you thought would bring you happiness and everything you believed was true has to be thrown away. Deep suffering in your soul clears the slate so that you can be built back up anew and true.

Before you can grow, before you can awaken to this better life, before you can wake up and live, period, you have to first acknowledge the state of perpetual disappointment that you have been living in. You have to admit that you have been settling for less than you deserve. Then, after you acknowledge this, you can work on coming to appreciate it, which usually takes a while longer.

The process is thorough, and it starts with becoming aware that something is desperately missing from your life. Your life lacks meaning, purpose, love, inspiration, joy, and peace. There is a hole in you. You will feel an emptiness inside of you, like a big hole in your heart; no amount of outside "happiness activities" seems to help. Following this emptiness will lead you down the rabbit hole. Your freedom awaits on the other side of that rabbit hole. Whether you have been through a dark night of the soul before or if you have witnessed someone else's suffering, then you know the feeling. Something fundamental to your core level of existence is off-balance, out of focus, or wholly lacking in your life. There is a vague sense while going through deep suffering that more is possible for your life. Even in the darkness, and even though you don't know exactly what it could be, you know that there is much more in store for you, and you want to discover what it is.

This simple drive to know your truest self is a facet of spiritual alchemy. Here, on your soul's journey along the path toward truth, you let go of your past self and embrace your highest self. Part of spiritual alchemy is something called 'solution' which is when you put all of the hard stuff into the waters of reflection so that it may dissolve. Your ideas, your habits, your thought patterns, and your false beliefs all break apart and melt away in these waters. This is your grand opportunity to start fresh.

For a while, you may feel like two people at once as your delusions about what you thought mattered begin to break down around you. There might be one part of you that is still chasing things outside of yourself in pursuit of happiness while another part of you is reaching for something new inside of yourself. One part is dying, and the other part is just beginning to truly live. Once your ego-self dies, you will begin to find and do the things that make you whole again.

Although it won't ever be easy, you have no choice but to trust that the darkness of suffering will lead your soul to a new dawn. The darkness of the night does not last forever. You will complete the journey, and you will become enlightened in the process. When you come through to the daylight, you will feel brand new. You will be able to help others find their way, too. You will recognize when they are going through perhaps their first experience of prolonged suffering, and you will be able to help them see through the darkness to the light of their new dawn.

When your soul journeys through struggle, it is an invitation to embrace the process of metamorphosis. It is a beckoning call to accept both deconstruction and resurrection into your life. You have to accept both. You have to anticipate the revival to survive the devastation. It is part of your soul's heroic journey through cycles of death and rebirth as you shed outdated ways of being and continuously and organically evolve into the most authentic version of yourself. Embrace the process. Some things need to die. The opportunity to navigate your soul's journey through suffering is a gift. You are given the chance to integrate your core wounds into a self-reclamation that results in the truest version of yourself.

When your soul journey brings you to a time of deep suffering, you might initially perceive the experience to be a period of significant loss—and indeed it probably is. You may lose loved ones, relationships, jobs, dignity, patience, or trust. You may lose a lot. Still, it is your job to know that in the end, the experience will result in an integrated, sovereign, and woke version of yourself. Through the darkness, all illusions will decompose and allow new ways of being to take root, and you will gain from the experience.

You will also evolve from the experience. Suffering and depression commonly occur when you bump up against your next threshold of evolution. These transitional areas contain a lot of energy which often manifests in the body and mind as confusion and suffering. It means you are evolving. You are adapting and responding to your physical environment, and you are thriving. It is a cornerstone of spiritual awakening. You need to embrace it when it comes, even if it takes some time before you realize what is happening.

Spiritual awakening is a precious gift that everyone deserves. Take advantage of it when it comes, even when it comes in the form of suffering. Trust that there is a passageway through for you to survive the darkness and deconstruction of your perceived reality. Trust your soul's journey of expansion and embodiment. As your soul expands, so too does your consciousness. Allow the cycles of death and rebirth. Allow your ego-self to die. Allow your higher self to emerge from the remains. Allow the darkness of struggle in your whole being to wrestle with you until the negative is purged from deep within you. Wrestle back. Wrestle with your fears. Wrestle with your personal conditioning. Wrestle free from these constraints as you strengthen yourself.

One of the great purposes of your soul's journey through suffering is to bring you to the light so you can access self-love and self-acceptance. This is true freedom, when ego-identification and the wounded parts of yourself are honored and welcomed back home rather than banished and shamed for their existence. When we are free of ego and suffering, there is more space, and we embody more love. This is expansion into a more conscious life. It requires tremendous courage to dismantle old belief systems and finally allow their falseness to be revealed so you can access the diamond within.

Remember, a diamond is a piece of coal that withstood millions of years of pressure to form. That diamond is you. It is all of you, and you are more than your name, more than your ego.

Your soul's journey matters to you and everyone you interact with. When these heavy questions surface along the way, allow your mind to extract the true meaning from them before delving into the quest for answers. As you read on, you will learn how your mind is built to sometimes divert attention away from your soul's journey in favor of your usual mental journey. The language that you think in becomes very important. Do your best to ask these questions in a slightly different way that opens up new possible responses. When you want to ask, "What is the point of life?" instead try, "Why must there be a point to life?" This language allows the experience of life itself to be reason enough, and it does not prompt you to look outside of yourself to find more than a moment can hold. This moment is enough. This current moment is reason enough for life to continue, for it contains all of the happiness you need and deserve.

Chapter 3

Why Does Suffering Happen?

Out of suffering have emerged the strongest souls; the most massive characters are seared with scars. – Kahlil Gibran

——— ··•·· ———

According to Buddhist teachings, our suffering arises from attachment to desires. These desires can vary from material objects, sensual pleasures or even relationships. The reason desiring causes suffering is because attachments are transient and loss is inevitable. If you expect one thing but receive another, you experience suffering. If you think things will go one way, and they go another way, you experience suffering. Anytime you have an expectation that is not met, you will suffer. That's what suffering is. Until you can live inside of each moment exactly as it is, you will experience suffering. You need to accept each moment as if you chose it.

You expect to be healthy. You expect to be satisfied. You expect to be treated with kindness. When these things are in any way unmet, you experience suffering.

Nothing evolves without encountering obstacles and then overcoming them. That is the whole of evolution. The environment presents an obstacle, and the fittest solution wins and survives. Wings evolved for certain creatures to escape danger and find food in higher locations. Feet evolved with a myriad of features like claws, hooves, and toes to traverse different terrains. The tongue evolved in more than one direction as an organ for digestion and language production so that creatures could eat and vocalize. These traits are favored in their respective environments because they foster survival.

Spiritual evolution is different from biological evolution in that you get to consciously decide to embrace the obstacles that manifest in your world and accept them as potential openings toward growth. You get to choose how to react to your challenges and how to move through your suffering.

You come to see soon enough that the only way through suffering is to accept it. Sometimes you can take action to sidestep or lessen the suffering. If your health is challenged, you can take steps to better your well-being. If your relationships suffer, you can work on the underlying issues. In any case, your best option is to treat the obstacle as if you chose it for yourself to force yourself into action. While it's always a good idea to improve your health and relationships, seldom do you initiate such change on your own, unprompted by challenges.

One thing that you should never do is give up and act as if nothing is possible. If you believe that there is nothing you can do, then there is nothing you can do, and you will suffer more for your hopelessness.

Suffering happens because life is a series of challenges to respond to. This is how you grow and expand into your best self. It happens to every human being, which is easy to see because it presents as obstacles. It also happens for every human being, which is more difficult to see. Because of the underlying feeling that accompanies suffering that life is constantly sabotaging your efforts to find happiness, it is hard to accept suffering into your life. It seems counterproductive.

But it is important to acknowledge that life is in the conspiracy for your growth.

Life is in the business of creating obstacles in the interest of your growth.

There is greatness at the other end of suffering. The initial blow that comes with suffering is fleeting if you know how to accept life's challenges. If you can look at it and not take it personally, then you will move through your suffering purposefully, enriching your soul with different experiences as you go. Of course, along the way, you will encounter many ego desires as you continue to shed this outdated part of yourself. Your past may come back to haunt you with the fallout from decisions you have made, and you may have to face the challenge that you thought you had already dealt with. Things tend to come back around in a layer-like fashion until you have completely shed them, one thin layer of skin at a time.

Understanding why suffering happens does not erase the suffering. Life will continue to throw you setbacks as you gain knowledge and insight into the purpose of suffering. It will manifest in many different ways to grow different parts of you. One challenge might require that you learn to take on another person's pain so that you can empathize better with their soul's experience. Another obstacle might present you with the chance to analyze yourself and see how you have mingled pleasure with pain in your mind before, so much so that you created a conditioned habit. You could also suffer an experience that is meant to bring you face to face with your deep, subconscious programming. Suffering takes many shapes and can piggyback its way into almost any situation for a multitude of reasons, and each time it is best met as a challenge for personal and spiritual growth.

It seems cliché to say, but it is nonetheless true that the level of suffering you experience depends upon how you see it and how you handle it. Your reaction is for you to decide.

This principle of suffering is seen in religious texts. One helpful comparison tool is the Bible. People of many faiths love to read this historical text. It illustrates many things, among them the human hunger for worship and the longing to communicate with the divine. When you go to God in this way, through religious writings and doctrines, it is not a sign of your maturity but a sort of courting phase between you and your spiritual journey. You are learning the language and symbolic structure of a soul's journey that is as ancient as time.

God, in the sense we will speak, means your higher power, whatever divine power you believe in and converse with. Maybe you call it "spirit" or "the Universe", or maybe you have no word for the force that acts in your life that you believe in. God, for these purposes, is meant to encompass any and all of these meanings.

The Bible speaks of a time when God will bid a person to grow deeper. It says God will remove the known comfort of the old version of your soul to teach you virtue and to grow you. This is the darkness of suffering in the soul and the process of your soul's evolution. The Bible says that Paul had a thorn in his side (whether it is literally true or not is unknown). However, God refused to remove this pain from Paul. He had to undergo a suffering process, and Paul's transformation came through his suffering.

When you are in the midst of a deep struggle on your journey, the words, books, and prayers of religious texts will mean nothing to you. The same pages that once enlightened you will leave you cold. You will cease to believe in all its wonder. Not everyone who enters exits in light, for not all are ready to heal.

Also in the Bible, Jesus Christ did not heal everyone he encountered who needed healing. Active participation of the person being healed was required. In the text, the Savior says that if a person does not believe, then they are not open to healing. Here, belief is seen as an active state of being for the healed individual, and they had the free will to decide whether to believe or not. Christ could not override that free will. If a person chose to not believe, then they were closed off to the healing Christ had to offer. He could not force healing on them, and their opposition caused them more struggle.

The same is true for you. Your soul's healing journey is yours alone to discover.

Remember, you are in a self-created box of walls that once protected you, but that is now keeping you from expanding into your highest self. Your soul wants peace. Some souls want to skip going through the hell that is deep, dark suffering. These souls seek transcendence and skip right over the darkness in reach of the light, and that is their journey. These souls believe that they do not have to suffer to find peace, and they make their home in the peace of non-suffering. Other souls who have experienced suffering and who seek to make sense of their pain from a spiritual perspective will go through that hell and darkness to find the true light they are after. These souls believe that they must go through suffering to find real and lasting peace. These souls will burn down every false fiber of their existence just to rise from the ashes, awake and grown.

Suffering also happens simply because of the physical body you inhabit. Sometimes, just having a physical body is enough to cause suffering. You suffer your physical body daily, especially in the head region with that thing called your brain. Your brain is a part of your body. Any mental suffering is inherently also physical. You suffer the weight of thoughts that attach to and attack your mind every day. You suffer the thoughts in your head that are actual things to be dealt with. You have to do work—actual mental and physical—work to grab ahold of your thoughts and reign them in. You have to learn that skill like taming a wild animal.

Not every symptom of suffering is negative. You will notice signs and coincidences everywhere. Little synchronicities will pop up in your day, and inexplicable things will happen that leave you with a small sense of being on the right track. While driving and thinking about your state, you suddenly might see a road-sign, or a banner on the roadside or a car plate number or a phrase; these may speak to your current mindset. You might notice an animal or a number or hear something that holds some level of significance for you. When the world sends you these signs, receive them as confirmation that you are right where you are supposed to be.

One of my earlier spiritual teachers coined the word 'blesson' to mean a blessing that is a lesson. A dark time of suffering in your soul is a blesson. Suffering is a blesson. All around you throughout your soul's journey are blessons beckoning you onward to the most evolved version of yourself that you can possibly inhabit. Pay attention to what comes to you during your darkest moments. Keep your eyes and ears open, and keep your mind quiet. So many people try to distract themselves by staying busy with meaningless or mindless activities that divert their attention away from their suffering. People plug their ears with devices and spend hours on their computers and phones searching outside of themselves for relief. They join every group and take up every cause to avoid themselves, and they never receive their blessons or become who they are really meant to be.

There is nothing inherently wrong with any of these distractions. Technology is useful. Having hobbies is fulfilling. Falling in love is exciting. Discovering your inner artist is inspiring. All of it has positive merit. The problem is when you focus on these things exclusively and leave your soul's journey on the back burner. When you get lost in your job, your passions, or your distractions, you temporarily relieve the suffering. While it is natural to want to alleviate your anguish, you do need to spend some time with it, too. Set it aside if you must, but come back to it willingly.

If you keep ignoring it, it will keep coming back. Suffering will manifest anywhere and everywhere. You might suffer loneliness, or you might suffer togetherness in an unsatisfying relationship. You might suffer from sickness, or you might be perfectly healthy and still suffer. You will still suffer whether you are affluent or in poverty. You will suffer whether you are comfortable or uncomfortable with your life. Suffering creeps through any crack until it settles in you, so you might as well accept it sooner rather than later.

It cannot be escaped. It cannot be ignored, smothered, or hidden with a smile.

Suffering is necessary. There is a term in psychology called "positive disintegration". By definition, positive disintegration is the idea that anxiety and tension are necessary components of spiritual growth. These create friction enough to scrape off the old parts of you and reveal the shiny, true version of you that was hidden beneath the surface. You have to look at yourself honestly and see what kind of life you have been settling for.

It is scary to look your disappointment in the eye and acknowledge it. A part of you might equate acknowledgment with acceptance, but these are two different things with their own distinct timelines. Acknowledgment makes you aware of a sense of incompletion that seems to be written into human programming. It makes you aware of what's absent in your life, what's lacking, and what's desperately missed. When you suffer greatly, these things come into full view as you start to desire more for your life and more from your life. Even if you are still in the dark about how and when your life's change will happen, you know you can't keep going the way you are.

In the world of mystics and mystical experiences, there is a concept known as the "halo effect" or 'afterglow', or what some refer to as the "sobriety of union." What you call it doesn't matter; what's important is the experience it speaks to as an explanation for why suffering is prolonged. You might catch a glimpse of the divine energy at work in your life. This sparks you on your soul's journey, but it fades from you. You lose the experience and are resubmerged into suffering.

Imagine yourself on a spectrum. At one end is you as you were existing before you embarked upon your soul's journey, and at the other end is you as you shall be when this phase of the journey is complete. One end is in darkness, and the other end is in the light. There is a lot of space between these two versions of you.

On the path toward your rediscovered, divine self, you move further away from your ego-self. There is a stark contrast between who you were and who you are becoming. If you feel the spark of divine influence in your life clearly, and you're not in a spiritually mature space yet, then the experience might stir up so much distress that it smothers the spark. This is the 'afterglow' in action. It happens when what you glimpse in the spark is so far away from where you are, and the path feels impossibly long. Now, when you're nearer the other end of the spectrum and more spiritually mature in your journey, the 'afterglow' acts more like a synchronous affirmation from the divine, cheering you on. Now, you know how to better navigate the path of transformation.

Chapter 4

When Does It End?

Our past may explain why we're suffering but
we must not use it as an excuse to stay in
bondage. – Joyce Meyer

—— ·· ● ·· ——

At first glance, the idea of a soul's journey might seem
destined to be full of peace and bliss. It sounds de-

lightful and promising. Then you experience agony, pain, discomfort, disease, and other various negative expressions, and you change your mind about whether a soul's journey is something you want to embark upon.

The only question you have at this stage is, "When will the suffering end?"

The positive and negative aspects of suffering are like opposite sides of the same coin, and you never know for sure which side will land face up or what kind of experience will come next. What you can count on is that life will continue to come at you in chunks of time known as moments. Whether you are a budding novice or have full mastery over what comes to be experienced, you create every moment.

As you start to get in touch with mortality, you necessarily question life. You might begin to grieve the loss of people in your life, people who are still alive but who have played a role in your suffering. Even your relationships suffer during this dark time of struggle.

When your whole being suffers this way, and you are drawn internally to examine yourself, the hardest part is to face your own shadow. Your shadow contains the repressed parts of yourself that you have not yet faced, that you have not yet dared to face. Your shadow is home to your fears, desires, traumas, and beliefs, and you need to go back home and confront them head-on. Draw courage from the knowledge that you are in a phase of spiritual growth that will not last forever.

Other questions that arise when you are in a deep state of suffering are existential and often unanswerable at that moment. Still, you will be compelled to ask yourself these questions many times:

These questions reflect a multitude of mental symptoms that accompany suffering. In the state of deep struggle, you will be tempted to abandon your journey and the seeming will of God. Because of your inability to sense God's presence in your life or believe in God's existence, you will feel alone and abandoned.

It will become difficult to have faith or seek out any goodness during such an unspecified period of suffering that feels endless. You will feel hopeless and without a purpose in life until you get through it.

You are justified in your feelings and desire to escape the darkness and suffering that your soul's journey has thrown you into. Life as you know it collapses. The perceived meaning of your life breaks down, and you are left with a deep sense of meaninglessness. When you enter into this phase, it often presents as a life-altering eruption of your reality, so of course you feel the way you feel. Your suffering is real.

It might take some time and the experience of getting through a period of deep suffering in your soul before you can see that you alone create the interference in your journey. You give your energy to the events that unfold in your journey, and this works both negatively and positively. You are the one who creates walls to hide safely behind. These barriers did at one time serve an important function, usually to protect yourself from being hurt in some way. As you heal, though, your work is to remove the walls and reintegrate the parts of yourself that were hurt once, twice, or many times before. Then, your suffering ends.

Mostly, this process happens unconsciously. You create an illusionary entity, an expectation, an image of truth in your mind's eye, and you believe it. Your brain tells you, "This person wants to hurt you", and you believe it because it is believable. After all, maybe you have been hurt by this person before. So, for that reason, you build up your wall one brick higher. It's not your brain's fault. Part of its function is to protect you so that you survive this lifetime—but if you let it run wild, it only creates more suffering because you now have to go through the experience of removing that brick.

You might have many walls that need to come down, though, and they are unique to you and your experience. No two people experience the same event in the same way. People are made up of a diverse web of emotional attachments, and even if you go through the exact same physical experience with them, you will not have the same emotional reaction or subsequent mental processing of that experience. Every soul's journey is distinct.

It is not an exact science. Sometimes, unfortunate things happen and there is no worldly explanation for them. Suffering cannot always be explained and must be experienced to be understood. When things of this nature happen, most likely karma is involved.

Karma is an energy. It's the energy of everything you've ever done in this lifetime and all others, and it plays a role in deciding your future incarnations. Karma is the energy of cause and effect.

You have probably heard someone say, "That happened because they had bad karma", to explain something unexplainable. It is common to attach the judgment of good or bad to karma to try to understand it, but the energy of karma is better understood in terms of negative and positive experiences. If you perform acts that have a positive nature, then your karma will reward you with more positivity. Likewise, if you are suffering a negative experience now, it is because you performed acts in a past life that were negative. In this case, your karmic energy needs to balance and heal. Until then, you will continue to manifest the same cycle of karma.

The karmic perspective offers at least three great features. One, bad karma can be overcome by goodwill. Karma does not leave you stranded and doomed forever. You can turn the energy back around. Two, there is no other way to realign your karmic energy than to endure what comes. There is no guesswork. The way to end karmic suffering is to suffer and then shed the layer of old existence that is ready to detach from your soul. Three, if you don't believe that you are capable of this kind of karmic healing by yourself, then you can trust a guru or enlightened, spiritual teacher—or Christ himself—to remove from you that which is allowed to be removed. Karma offers these tools to assist your soul's journey.

There are three broad categories of karma:

1. The karma that can be overcome or transformed by goodwill.

2. For some types of karma, your spiritual teacher or guru or an enlightened being has the ability to dissolve or remove, but for which the removal does not take away your lessons.

3. Another type of Karma is something that one has to experience; there is no way to avoid it.

How you choose to go through life is up to you, and any way you choose, you will undoubtedly run into troubling obstacles along the journey. Good karma will not save you from obstacles or speed up your journey from suffering to healing. Positive thinking is helpful, but it also will not free you from encountering obstacles. Your soul needs to experience the consequences of your past actions so that you can understand how your own mind contributed to your suffering.

In hindsight, will you look back and be grateful for your struggles? Your personal and spiritual growth is worth it. In essence, no pain, no gain. If you aren't sufficiently bothered by your repetitive thoughts, then you won't take action to change them. If you don't see that your mind is limiting your fullest expression by keeping you safe in hiding, then you can't move through it. Going through it is growth, and it comes with disturbance, pain, and suffering. All of it is a blessing in disguise, so welcome it when you recognize it, and take an active role in your soul's evolution.

Chapter 5

How Does Suffering Manifest?

Every adversity, every failure, every heartache carries with it the seed of an equal or greater benefit. – Napoleon Hill

·———· ·· ● ·· ·———·

S uffering manifests in many different forms across the body, mind, and environment. More and more, people and professionals recognize the connection between the mind and the body, between thoughts and disease. They are connected, and they manifest both externally and internally. They come into your reality from the outside environment, and they're born into your reality from inside. The world is a beautiful canvas, and you are a powerful creator.

External manifestations can be tricky to conceive of properly. There is an easy way to understand this kind of manifestation, and there is a harder way. The easy way to think about external manifestation is that it is suffering caused by the environment. Maybe your relationship with someone in your physical environment is causing strife. It's coming from outside of you. It could also be manifesting as a result of an interaction with something from outside of yourself. This is the harder way to think about external manifestations. This is the grief that you feel from your strained relationship. This is the anxiety that you feel from an overactive mind or from worrying about a particular issue. This is your general discomfort from physical ailments that plague your body. This is your depression, your loneliness, your sadness. It's also your headaches from the constant stress and frustration that your physical being suffers.

Internal manifestation is the same sort of negative experience except that it comes from an internal catalyst. Where external is about coming into contact with something outside of yourself, internal is about manifesting suffering from something you created internally. If you inhabit a state of constant, deep longing, you will manifest from this space and invite more of the same into your experience. If you have an unhealthy attachment to something—a fixation or an addiction—then you will suffer in layers. You will suffer when your expectation is unmet, and then you will suffer a period of self-blame and judgment, and then you will suffer the repeated creation of attachment in your reality. If you create from a space of want, you create more want.

In some cases, the source of your suffering is beyond your conscious comprehension. The subconscious mind is at play here. The subconscious is the storehouse of all deep conditioning and emotional thought patterns. The habits and attitudes are a reflection of what is in your store-house. Our school and society teach us very little about how to determine what is stored in our subconscious minds. Although this is beyond the scope of this book, one effective way that the subconscious mind reveals the nature of stress/ suffering is through dreams and visions. Dreams are a window to your soul. The more you start paying attention to your dreams, your intuition will begin to draw more and more from your subconscious into your conscious state. This can potentially reveal the source of your stress. Your healing can then follow.

You can start to see how suffering manifests from internal states and external encounters. The characteristics of suffering make sense as these two entries into suffering interact and entangle. Something happens, and it disturbs your peace inside. You lose sleep at night because you're up thinking about all of the possible outcomes of the situation. You lose interest in your life. You lose friends or family or a loved one. You lose your faith, and it takes a toll on your physical, mental, and emotional health. You become introverted, and all of your energy turns inward, creating a schism between your inner and outer world. This draws you in further, into a life of duality where you suffer even to the point of thoughts of suicide just to relieve the suffering. As your body and mind suffer new and more ailments, you curse God and the higher beings for betraying you. You curse your existence.

This time is super-charged with emotions and longing for it all to end. The more you wish it would end, the more your physical ailments seem to manifest. This creates a lot of anger, and anger is one of the biggest underlying causes of illness in the body. Sometimes anger is overlooked as a potential cause of illness because it is invisible. It's easier to try to pinpoint a tangible cause than accept that a repressed emotion is to blame. In this way, people form attachments to the answers they want to be true, but the answers are often complex and difficult to interpret. It helps if you are able to pay more attention to what is raging inside of you and less attention to what is going on outside and around you. It is not a time to ignore yourself or try to escape yourself, but a time to listen to what your body is telling you.

More on this will come later in the discussion of healing yourself, but the emotional and psychological underpinnings of physical ailments are enlightening to consider. Bodily pain is closely tied to all other experiences, physical, mental, emotional, and spiritual. What you feel in one part of your body manifests across all parts of your body in some way. One way to make sense of a foot injury, for example, is to interpret its meaning as being that you are headed in the wrong direction. Or if you have hemorrhoids, it's an ailment of being unable to release toxicity from within. If your spine is out of alignment, your very foundation is suffering, or possibly even your life is on the line. The literal and abstract meanings intertwine for a new picture of illness that threads together your internal state of being and external manifestations.

When this happens and the worlds outside and inside feel too tumultuous for you to go on, you will most likely believe that God has abandoned you. This is the timeless shape that suffering takes, and as illogical as it seems, this is when you need God the most. This is the point when you have given up and God no longer walks beside you but carries you onward instead.

The good news is that the universe is an endless source of new opportunities, and you can grab hold of any one of them and get yourself through any dark night of the soul. In the moment, it might seem easier to suppress what is coming up and pretend that it doesn't exist or it's not happening, but this will only manifest later in emotional turmoil. If you don't do the work to let the past stir in you so that you can let go of the pain attached to it, then your emotional baggage will continue to carry itself into your present and future lives.

Before we change gears and discuss your soul's metamorphosis in more detail, it's worthwhile to highlight a few vital points. First, internal and external manifestations are very different. They can evoke similar outcomes, but their source is what matters, and they come from two very different places.

Second, a good analogy to keep in mind while going through the darkness of deep suffering in your soul is that you are like a boxer fighting for your life in the ring. You might feel barely alive, and as though life is still, constantly creating more obstacles for you. You are fighting against your life as you've created it up to that point, and you are fighting for the life you deserve. You're barely recognizable at this point as you have mentally checked out of reality for a bit. You could be surrounded by people, but your presence is elsewhere in your mind and not with your present company. Your physical self will be there, people will see you, but your conscious self will be elsewhere.

Third, some people turn toward and rely heavily upon religion when their soul suffers. You can become esoteric in your beliefs as a way to allow religion to rescue you. The best part of this habit is that you have begun your spiritual journey, and you are now a seeker of knowledge. The part of religion that you should release, however, is the belief that one doctrine's way is the only way through suffering. Go to religion for knowledge, not for absolute truth.

Comparison in general is not helpful on this journey. If you truly understand that suffering is a blessing in disguise, then it should not matter what form it comes in for you or anyone else. You cannot judge another person's suffering even if it appears as if you have experienced the same thing they are going through. You understand that the same things can manifest for different reasons, so turn your attention away from others and back to your own soul's journey.

A fourth note to remember is that there are a few things that will always help and a few things that will never help when you are suffering through dark times in your soul. Keep your attention on the things that you love: maybe there is only one thing that you can still feel love for in this state of suffering, but if you spend more time where you feel good, it will always help. If it feels good to rest, rest. If it feels good to walk, walk. If it feels good to create something, create something. Take care not to create more suffering with excessive escape or unhealthy outlets, but do find moments of release when you can. But remember, you need to sit with your suffering, too. Don't simply ignore it.

You can do both at the same time. You can embrace the suffering you're experiencing while also seeking relief from it. The outdoors is a great tool for this. One conscious breath outside is like medicine for your soul. Breathe it in. In this way, you allow yourself to be in the depressed emotional state you find yourself in while staying present in the moment. This is good practice.

Finally, it cannot be overstated that you must hold onto hope. At all costs, have hope. You are being molded and shaped into a better version of yourself. Allow it to happen, but know that there will come a time when you find yourself on the other side of suffering. Know that you are in waiting mode, holding onto the promise of God. You might lose sight of God, but humble yourself with the knowledge that your sight is limited when going through a dark night of the soul. Your sight is upgrading.

From personal experience, the period spent waiting is a frustrating time, and you will struggle to hear your intuition and use discernment. You will feel like there is something inside of you that is trying to kill you, and the more you push back on it, the more it pushes you back. You will feel moments of a deep sense of not belonging where you are. You will be very upset a lot of the time. You will still want to live your past life as the self that you knew and were used to. You will want to cling to your old life and try to deny the imminent death coming to claim that old life. You will go to new places and find new jobs, but this deep unrest will keep you from feeling like you belong there, and joy and gratitude will elude you in new settings. You will quit jobs because of this feeling. You will choose solitude because of this feeling. You will think you had everything you ever wanted, and you will beat yourself up for being unhappy and ungrateful. You will be shaken from your usual limited perception of life, and what will stir up are intense feelings of sadness, frustration, hope-lessness, and meaninglessness. You will experience some-thing you've never been through before: a homesickness for a place that never was, known as a hiraeth.

You will feel the painful shedding of previous concep-tual frameworks as things begin to fall away. Your identity, your relationships, your career, habits, and beliefs will all flake off and die. You will feel it all. Your faith will flicker, as Ram Dass puts it. You will lose your sense of self and gain distrust in others. You won't know who you really are or what you want from life. You will wander in the dark until your faith flickers again. Anchor to that spark of light as you allow your old self to say goodbye to the outdated constructs of meaning in your life. This is how you will create space for a new version of you to expand.

Your grief might come in the form of a loved one's death, or it could be catalyzed by a different sort of loss in your life. In it, you will start down one path that feels like it might help, but it often doesn't, so you will have to turn and try another path. Every time you have to change gears, it takes so much energy for you to try again, and you might want to give up. It goes like this, on and on, with you collapsing in despair only to somehow rise again. It's like your mind is frozen. It's stuck. It keeps trying to move you in a certain direction that used to work for you, and it keeps not working this time. Cycling through this is tormenting. By the end, you can barely still feel that last thread of hope in the palm of your hand. Somehow, you manage to listen to the inchoate part of you that believes you will know deep, satisfying joy one day.

Even though the problem is in your mind, the problem is not your mind. The solution is not your mind, either. Your mind is conditioned, that's what it knows. It just needs to be retrained. It needs to be quieted down, soothed, recalibrated to a higher frequency, and then invited along on your soul's journey as a worthy companion, not as the sole decision maker.

Your mind is the product of evolution. It has developed to protect you from danger and keep you alive. It structures your existence and becomes the lens through which you view and interpret life's experiences. It does what it does very well, but it can't be expected to do everything. It simply cannot do everything. To come to terms with your dark night of the soul, you must understand that the mind is limited. It is bound by its conditioning, but it is also completely fickle and reprogrammable. It is a multi-purpose tool.

Since its ability is limited, the mind's reasoning and logic are also limited. It so badly wants to answer the questions you run through it. It wants to answer you when you ask,

"What's the point of life?" It wants to search and find the answer like a good student, and it wants to please you by finding the answer that brings you happiness—but it goes about things in the default and usual ways. Your mind has focused heavily on gathering information from outside of itself and needs to build up its inventory of self-knowledge and self-wisdom. Then your manifestations will be better constructed from a place of conscious intention that serves your soul's journey.

Psychosomatic Issues

When we experience a dark night of the soul, our bodies undergo much physical stress. This is because our emotions and our physical bodies are intrinsically linked. One affects the other and vice versa. Most of us have heard this said before. When you get a bad headache or you start breaking out in acne or rashes, your loved ones may ask, "do you think it could be stress?" More likely than not, the answer is yes, even if you don't realize it at the moment. Our emotions play a massive role in our overall physical wellbeing. When you're feeling good on the inside, you're probably feeling good in your body as well.

Dr. Susan Bell, a psychologist who specializes in trauma-induced depression, believes that when we feel a frequent amount of stress or anxiety, we actually debilitate our bones over an extended amount of time. According to her, our muscles are actually restricted and stressed when our minds are stressed as well. When our bones are tense for too long, they enter a state of more permanent debilitation. This is why some people suffer with prolonged back pain or other physical pains. It's a message from the body saying, "I need to be free. I need to relax." A dark night of the soul can prompt these feelings with frequent intensity.

According to pain experts, around 15-30% of patients reporting chronic pain have a history of Post-Traumatic Stress Disorder (PTSD). This makes sense since, as I stated previously, our bodies and our minds are intrinsically connected. Therefore, if you've endured prolonged abuse or mistreatment, your body will remember it. And when your mind is triggered once again, your body will react similarly. Scientists now have reason to believe that certain specific symptoms represent certain specific stressors. Let's explore what each of these are...

Headaches are said to be a result of the everyday stresses in our lives. Migraines, for example, may be a sign that your everyday routine or practices are causing stress on your mind and body. If you find that you experience an excessive number of headaches during your suffering process, see if there's a way you can adjust your routine. Create more space for relaxation and activities that bring you peace and happiness. A change in routine could very well alleviate your head's pain.

If you're experiencing pain in your neck or throat, scientists believe that it may be a sign you have trouble with forgiveness. Essentially, it may be difficult for you to forgive those around you, or even yourself. If you're holding on to grudges or you're carrying a lot of animosity toward the people in your life, your neck may feel the effects. Make sure that you aren't being too hard on yourself. Practice forgiveness and see if your neck and throat experience a release with your newfound grace.

If you carry a lot of pain in your shoulders, it could be a sign that you are metaphorically carrying the weight of the world on your back. Maybe you internalize the pain of others, or try to save people without giving yourself the same patience and attention. In the same vein, pain in the upper back may suggest that you are craving love or emotional support in some way. Lower back pain reflects a similar issue, but it's more related to financial or worldly stress. There are also more acute pains that point to very specific internal hang-ups. For example, elbow pain is said to reflect a resistance or fear of change. And if you experience pain in your palm, it could mean you find it hard to reach out to others for support. Perhaps you need to find the courage to lean on others more.

If you're experiencing pain in your hips, that could be a sign that you're afraid of forward momentum. Maybe you want to move ahead in life, but you fear the results or what will happen in the process. Look out for hip pain, for it may be a reflection of your perceived, stunted progress. Alternatively, if you suffer from chronic knee pain, it may be a sign that your ego needs a rebirth--which is especially common during the dark nights of your soul journey. And if you suffer from liver problems, it could mean that you have an unhealthy relationship with anger. Similarly, issues with the lungs may reveal unexpressed or unacknowledged grief. Heart and brain issues may reflect problems with too much worrying, and kidney problems are reportedly a result of too much fear.

No matter what physical ailment you may be suffering with, there is research that points to a specific mental root. It may be wise to search the internet for what kind of mental stressors may be affecting your physical body. That way, you can get to the source of the issue and figure out what it says about your soul's journey as well. If you're experiencing increased back pain during your dark night of the soul, for example, your soul's journey may have themes of self-love and acquiring the love that you deserve. The mind, body and spirit are all connected. We tend to become more aware of this during the dark night of the soul.

So, once you understand the source of your symptoms, once you know the root and understand why stress or depression have wreaked havoc on your psyche, what can you do to alleviate the pain? What are the steps you can take to restore peace in your mind and body? The good news is there are several ways you can restore internal harmony, practices that you can start implementing today in order to gain some stability and solace amidst the chaos. The first involves creating a strong life philosophy for yourself.

Chapter 6

Suffering is Your Metamorphosis

Healing from pain is a choice. You have to
consciously decide that you deserve to feel
free, that you deserve to let go of the weight
that has been holding you down for too long.
– Sylvester McNutt III

Every life is unique, and every soul's journey is a once-in-a-lifetime experience of finding purpose. Depending on your purpose as a soul in this lifetime, you will have a set of deep desires that are meant to lead you in the direction of your soul's highest expression. This path is tied directly to your suffering as you go through different phases of striving toward your desires and are met with obstacles.

The most common metaphor for metamorphosis is the caterpillar that turns into a butterfly. Two completely different creatures are tied together by a process perfected by nature. Stage by stage, the caterpillar transforms into the winged version of itself. This process of re-birthing is a great analogy to what happens to your soul during suffering. The caterpillar is born with everything it needs, internally and externally, to become the butterfly. You are born with everything you need, inside of you and in your outside world, to become the next version of yourself. The caterpillar suffers a death of itself inside the cocoon. This is the same shedding you do when you pass through a dark time of suffering in your soul and reboot to your true self.

A lot happens when you pass through your cocoon stage of metamorphosis, but it doesn't always look like a lot is happening. From the outside, your life might appear to remain the same, but from the inside, your life is changing in ways that no one sees, not even you. On a spiritual level, your communication channels begin to open up during this phase. This means that your intuition starts to develop to facilitate communication with yourself, and you may become aware of your spiritual guides and mentors and begin to communicate with them. The more you open to the process, the louder the small voice inside of you becomes. That voice, by the way, has always been there—metamorphosis brings you awareness of it, but it has always existed. The difference is that now you can no longer ignore it. As your spiritual growth increases through the alchemy of suffering, you change in unseen ways.

The dark moments that you go through while in your cocoon will also bring many breakthroughs, and each one inches you toward enlightenment. The cycle that seems so torturous is actually leading you through the cocoon phase. Remember, you need to suffer to strengthen your new wings. You need to come to a point where nothing is working anymore, and you feel you have no choice. Spiritual leader, Eckhart Tolle, teaches that you have three choices: change the situation, leave the situation if you can't change it, or accept the situation as it is. If you can adopt this last stance and accept what's happening, then you can detach from your suffering and move through it.

It is not easy to change your thinking this way, to view the situation from a higher perspective, so you must practice.

Inside your cocoon, you will become aware of many things. You will start to understand universal laws like the law of cause and effect. It says that every action has a resulting consequence. It means that every time you do something, a similar occurrence is created. Positive actions result in positive circumstances. If you tell someone they are beautiful, they react with a smile and a feeling of joy. When you view your relationships with this law in mind, you will see the people in your life differently. They are helping you along. Your partner, family, and friends are your greatest teachers because they push your buttons and make you move from where you are to the next step.

As your awareness expands, you experience consciousness in a new way and begin to understand that consciousness is experience. When you are conscious of the moment, you are in the experience, evolving with the universe and its obstacles. You are right where you're supposed to be.

Metamorphosis is a blessing in the dark. It will detach you from all of your attachments that cause you great suffering. Attachment can take many forms. You can be attached to what other people think of you, and you will suffer their criticisms. You can be attached to anger and the need for battle, and you will be met with more negative emotions and actions. Anger creates suffering. Battle creates suffering. Defiance and denial create suffering. Anything of a similar density to anger, such as guilt or hatred, creates suffering in the body and mind.

In the case of the caterpillar and butterfly, there is a clear change in bodily form. In the case of your metamorphosis, there is a clear change in mentality and a refurbished connection between the body and the mind. The body becomes a clear reflection of the mind.

One way this is evident is with a disease. If a disease was caused by an emotionally imbalanced underpinning, then it must be cured with emotional balancing. If your poor self-image was the true cause of your skin condition, for example, then the cure is to fix your self-image. Health challenges are often used as obstacles in dark times of deep suffering. Diseases will manifest and persist, urging you onward to understand how they got there in the first place. In this way, illness in the body is like a cosmic telegram, sending information about your underlying emotional blocks, fears, and insecurities that are causing sickness in you. Your intuition improves during this time to help you listen to this internal communication.

Your metamorphosis is as unique as the rest of your soul's journey. Inside your cocoon, you will be shaped and molded into who you truly desire to be. You will struggle until you accept what is happening and detach from it: when you remember that suffering is happening for you, not to you. You are not a victim of suffering. The victim persona is outdated and must fall away, too. Nothing is happening to you. It is all happening for you to transform yourself and create happiness for yourself. This, too, is a job that requires a unique set of gifts and talents that only you have.

In this transitory state, you may feel like you are the only one who can save yourself, which may increase your feelings of loneliness and confusion about the world. It may feel endless, but there is an end to your suffering if you are equipped with the tools and knowledge you need to persevere to the next phase of your soul's journey.

Evolutionarily, every living creature that evolves into a higher form must forfeit its known existence. You must completely change your makeup. Allow the suffering in your soul to take from you what no longer serves your journey. Let your old beliefs and perspectives be shaved away. Forfeit your ego-self for the sake of your spiritual evolution. Trying to avoid the hard work of extinguishing an entire lifetime and deconstructing the constraints of the old structures that held you in place is futile and goes against the goal of the experience. The process of going through a dark time of suffering is what builds your true, authentic nature and allows you to embody your higher self.

Inside the cocoon, it is dark and cramped. The space feels wholly unsuited for growth, and emerging from it requires intervention from a higher power. This divine force is not called upon to save you or to rip you from the darkness before you're formed into yourself as intended. A higher power is needed to push you to strengthen yourself while in darkness so that you are strong enough to get yourself through. You won't receive God's help in removing obstacles. Instead, God will set the scene for you to root deeper inside yourself so that you can withstand anything that comes your way. This is true transformation. Your soul's suffering contains all aspects of your growth. It is the darkness where you sacrifice your sight to develop other senses. It is every opportunity to sharpen your intuition, empathy, and compassion. It is the fire that destroys your old way of life, and it is the flood of freshwater to revive your tired soul.

In Christianity, Jesus Christ is a symbol of metamorphosis. He dies on the cross, then is resurrected. Without suffering or death, there is no resurrection. This could be seen as a metaphor for letting your ego-self die so that you may transform. Jesus' suffering brought him closer to God. It was his calling to suffer, to bear the cross, to go through pain, and then to receive healing in his soul and be transformed in body. This was his awakening.

Spiritual awakening is priceless. It implies an enormous amount of change on every level of your being, and it can be terrifying. It's nowhere you've ever been before, so it's scary. It stirs fear, and also extinguishes it in the process. It's worth every horrible moment and every stumble in the darkness.

Awakening happens in many ways. Some people follow an enlightened spiritual teacher and trust that will awaken their soul. Other people have a strong spiritual drive to do the work themselves. Some people are spontaneously awakened by life's experiences. Any experience can be the source; there are no qualifying criteria. You can be launched into spiritual awakening by an illness, a breakup, a loss, a near-death experience, a war, a wedding, a book, a conversation, or a random thought. Whatever wakes you up, be grateful for it.

In theory, this seems easy enough, but in practice, it is very difficult to express gratitude when you are shrouded, emptied, and ushered into a dark period of suffering in your soul. At that moment, gratitude is the furthest thing away. Fill your head with theory, now, so that when you are in practice, you will automatically know what to do. You will know that whatever experience it is that wakes you up, it is happening to grow you. It is happening to rip you from your blind disappointment and open your eyes to parts of yourself that are still waiting to shine. When these pieces of you have been unearthed, polished, and integrated into your life, then you will be grateful for every moment you suffered.

Changing life philosophies

Life philosophies give us a framework to rely on. They put our primary values into focus, and ensure that we always have principles to lean on when everything else in life grows blurry or confusing. Our values take on new importance during dark nights of the soul. This is because our egos and previous attachments go through a dissolving period. The dark nights usually begin with some form of loss. We lose those things which we previously depended on for safety and security, and we're challenged to redefine ourselves according to new structures. This requires a reassessment of core values. If we previously put a lot of value on financial stability, for example, then the life lesson may bring a loss of a loved one, we may decide that money is not as important as time with friends and family. You may shift your values according to this newfound wisdom.

Our values form the foundation of our life philosophies. My own dark nights of suffering led me to reconsider my values in a major way, which also resulted in a new life philosophy. At the start of my dark times, my partner left for Spain to go to grad school. My roommate and my best friend also moved for grad school in the same year, and I was suddenly isolated. These were the people I spent all my time with, and just like that, they were gone. Their absence left an emptiness in its wake. I realized that I had invested too much of my own security and happiness into my relationships with others. Once they were gone, I had little of my own life to fall back on. I had relied on them for fun, social fulfilment, artistic inspiration, financial security, and many more facets of my life. Suddenly, I was challenged to take charge of my own happiness. I couldn't rely on others to provide it for me. At the same time, I learned that I had to embrace change. I had to be okay with the fact that some people wouldn't stay in my life forever, and that's okay.

This led me to a total shift in personal values. Before my dark night of the soul, I was obsessed with marriage. I'd panic if anyone close to me even suggested taking an extended vacation, or leaving me alone for too long. But with my loved ones' absence, I realized that I actually value my freedom a lot. I discovered that I could work remotely and travel to visit all of my friends without being obsessed with roots or stability. I found myself again through travelling and dating casually--this time, without all the hang-ups about marriage and the future. I discovered that if I just lived in the present, I could enjoy life and relish in the now. I don't have to care what happens in the future, I decided. And that changed everything for me. These are the kinds of revelations that dark nights of the soul promise. They give us a rich opportunity to realign our values from a more evolved state of mind.

We all need a life philosophy, because philosophies provide meaning. They point to a personal truth which quiets all the chaos and grounds us when everything else is upside down. "Without a philosophy of life, you may be swamped by your emotions and believe that life is meaningless. You see the chaos in and around you, and you assume that it could never make sense. With this attitude it is easy to latch onto simplistic explanations, which are never far away." Your life philosophy should be personal to you and your values. It shouldn't reflect the life philosophy of anyone else. It needs to come from your own intuition. It may take some time before you fully embody your new philosophy, and that's okay. You can't rush the process. But take the time to be honest with yourself. Realize that the dark times heralds a transformation. You may be surprised that you want things that are completely different than what you wanted before. But that's natural! You're not the same person you were before. So, feel all of your emotions, consider what you've learned through your dark night, and then reassess your values. With your new life philosophy, life will never be as scary as it was before your metamorphosis.

Chapter 7

Finding the Gifts in Darkness

We rarely find people who achieve great things without first going astray. —— Meister Eckhart

———— ·•●•· ————

Y ou come to the darkness to resolve your personal set of circumstances. No matter what desires drove you there or what obstacles slowed you down, you encounter suffering for the purpose of balancing your soul's karmic existence. This is the gift of suffering. You gain freedom through the darkness.

There is a distinct possibility that you emerge from darkness into a transformed state of consciousness. On the other side of suffering, life has meaning again. It's no longer a conceptual meaning, though, it's not something you can necessarily explain either. Its meaning is much deeper than you can readily access with your mind, and it brings a profound sense of purpose and connectedness with a life that is greater than you've ever experienced. Your life is no longer dependent upon the things you used to think were important. Your rebirthed self is different.

Your soul's suffering is a kind of death. Parts of you have died. The previous version of you is dead. The egoic sense of self is extinguished, and your truest self has emerged.

Like many other people who endure this transformation, you come through the darkness and realize that you had to suffer to experience your spiritual awakening. The suffering was part of your awakening; it was part of your strengthening. It was a time of great struggle where you amassed a wealth of knowledge and self-discovery.

The darkness that your soul journeys through contains many gifts. This stage of personal development causes you to undergo a significant transition to a deeper understanding of your life and your place in it. These are valuable gifts on your soul's journey. The struggle you confronted when you faced your shadow and all of the repressed parts of yourself had meaning. The fears, desires, traumas, and beliefs that broke through from inside of you and rippled out into your reality to be resolved all have meaning. They all come with a great reward—for as painful as your suffering has been, the fruition is unbelievably empowering and liberating.

A time of dark suffering in your soul is not a problem that you have to solve. Sometimes, you will get a peek at the darkness within you and think that you have to eradicate it. Maybe you tell someone or bring it up in therapy, and you reason through it until you can put it out of your mind and feel relief that it is over. It isn't over, and it hasn't even begun. Your ego-self wants to control your relationship with darkness, but it has no power over your soul or your soul's journey. If you are given a glimpse into your shadow, take it for what it is and allow it to exist. Sit with it, don't run away from it.

The weight of what your shadow holds is oppressive and holding you down, and relief from the pressure is not always easy to come by. You might begin by looking for help outside of yourself because this is what you have been trained to do in your human existence thus far.

Remember, your suffering is not for God, nor does it serve God. The suffering is for you and will serve you and everyone you interact with by extension. Everyone who experiences a deep struggle in their soul creates their own answer to the question of why it happens. No one's answer is right, and no one's answer is wrong. All solutions are the ego's and mind's attempt to create meaning out of chaos, which is what they're good at doing.

Your suffering is the epitome of a blessing in disguise. Wrapped in darkness and depression, it removes the ground from beneath your feet and leaves you to experience suffering in your soul. It leaves you there, illuminating the parts of you that are fearful, fragile, decaying, and in desperate need of change and growth. When it tries to claim these things from you, it only leaves you feeling more empty inside. Then, from somewhere deep in that dark void, from nowhere that ever existed before, from the mere potential of a shred of hope, a new seed is planted in you. This seed contains the true peace and joy that come from being aligned with your soul's purpose, and then you know you are blessed.

People can endure unimaginable ordeals and still manage to discover their talents and contribute to humanity's progress in a striking way. History provides many examples of exemplary individuals who suffered greatly—or who suffered in any capacity at all—and still went on to use their gifts to achieve greatness.

Abraham Lincoln is one outstanding example. His early life was surrounded by death and loneliness, and his adult life was weighed down by war and the death of thousands of young soldiers. He was known to be a melancholic man who suffered through the darkness, and still, he became an icon of wisdom and leadership. One theory says that the efforts he made for his country were what helped him escape his melancholy. Another idea is that the darkness itself was the ground upon which he grew his leadership. Either way, he once said, "If there's a worse place than hell, I'm in it."

Nelson Mandela is another strong example of someone whose suffering did not deter his significance. He was imprisoned for 27 years under harsh conditions, yet he never lost his vision or sense of destiny. A younger prisoner who knew Mandela said of him, "...he has a tremendous presence, apart from his bearing, his deportment, and so on. He's a person who's got real control over his behavior. He is also quite conscious of the kind of seriousness he radiates."

Maya Angelou is another intriguing example of how a dark time of suffering in the soul leads to a transformative presence in the world. As a child, she did not speak for a period of a few years. Her guilt and wounds of abuse kept her silent. As an adult, she recited the inaugural poem for President Bill Clinton, and her words inspired millions to make something of their soul's suffering. In all of her public appearances, she showed both the pain and the joy that shaped her mission in life. She carried her pain with her throughout her life, yet her joy seemed to increase with her impact on people from around the world. In her suffering and metamorphosis, she had her voice taken away from her and then returned with added strength and magnitude.

J.K. Rowling is another shining example. When she was trying to pitch Harry Potter and the Philosopher's Stone, she was on government assistance with young children. She was broke. She couldn't afford to make copies of her book to send out to publishers. Instead, she manually re-typed every single copy of the lengthy novel. She was rejected dozens of times, but she never gave up, and you know how that story ends: Rowling went on to become the first self-made billionaire author.

Jim Carey has led a transformational life, too. When he was 14 years old, his father lost his job, and his family became impoverished. Carey moved to Los Angeles when he was 16 years old to take a chance on his acting dreams. He wrote himself a fake check for $10 million to inspire himself to never give up, and he kept it with him in his wallet. It took him another 16 years before starring in his first hit movie, Dumb and Dumber. His father was the one who encouraged him to follow his dream, and when he died, Carey buried the fake check with him in his casket.

Oprah Winfrey is a great example of perseverance as well. Growing up, she was a victim of sexual abuse. Despite her incredibly challenging upbringing, she was an honors student in high school and earned a full scholarship to college. She didn't stop there: She climbed her way up the television network world and is one of the wealthiest people in the world and one of the most influential icons.

Michael Jordan is arguably the greatest basketball player of all time. He was once cut from his high school basketball team, but he never quit, he just worked harder. His desire was stronger than anything else. Jordan went on to become an NCAA star, a six-time NBA champion, an MVP in multiple leagues, and he was inducted into the Basketball Hall of Fame.

John F. Kennedy also endured sustained suffering before becoming a cultural icon. In his youth, before anyone knew of him as the President of the United States, Kennedy suffered a plethora of physical illnesses including chronic back pain. His health was poor, so he had to sneak his way into the US Navy to fight during World War II. He survived this and more on his soul's journey.

Mother Teresa of Calcutta is another example of someone who endured the darkness of deep suffering in her soul for decades. According to her letters, life was a struggle for her. She could not easily embrace the soul's journey, and this was during a time when there was much less discussion circulating about such spiritual matters. The darkness in her soul captured her after she found her "call within a call" and began her mission to serve the poorest of the poor in Calcutta, India. After hearing the call and receiving its message, she was still unable to feel the presence of God in her life. Through her suffering, she continued to follow God's will but also questioned the very existence of that God. In one of her letters, published in her book, Come Be My Light, Mother Teresa wrote, "In my soul, I feel just that terrible pain of loss—of God not wanting me—of God not being God—of God not really existing." Her journey of persevering faith is considered one of the longest recorded instances of a dark night of the soul.

Eckhart Tolle is an exemplary model of a contemporary spiritual healer and leader. He turned the experience of his own inner turmoil into a career as an author and teacher who has reached millions of people with his transformative work.

He thinks of deep suffering as a breakdown of the superficial meaning of life. It explodes into your life, covering everything with meaninglessness. An external event triggers it, and everything in your life that was meaningful collapses inexplicably. He also says it feels like depression. The true disaster is the collapse of the conceptual frameworks that held your life together formerly. These are the meanings that your mind ascribes to different facets of your life. They all cave in and you're left in the dark with the rubble. But you go into the suffering with the definite possibility that you will also come out of it, and life takes on a different sort of meaning that is not easily communicated in the usual language of conceptual thinking. You are re-birthed with greater connectedness, detached from your egoic sense of self. It is a death, and death is painful.

Of course, you can collapse old conceptual meanings in other ways that don't include great suffering. The very first lesson in A Course in Miracles, a popular spiritual self-help program, is to intentionally collapse the meanings of life that your mind made up. You practice by looking at different objects in the room and saying, "This doesn't mean anything, that doesn't mean anything". This is a small, benign rehearsal compared to the forced collapse of deep suffering, but it does help you understand the working and reworking of your mind.

Additionally, there is a story in the bible, in the book of Corinthians, where Paul is afflicted by a thorn in his flesh. At the peak of his highest height, he is stabbed by an incurable thorn. He pleaded with God to remove it. According to the bible, he did this at least three times, but God couldn't remove it. Removing it would eradicate the lesson that Paul was meant to learn, the lesson of grace. According to the passage, God stated, "My grace is sufficient for you, for my power is made perfect in weakness." Later, in Romans, Paul utters the sentiment that neither "height nor depth" can "separate us from the love of God in Christ." So, you see how there's a symbolic suggestion here. Paul's story illuminates something about the soul's journey and purpose. His story suggests something about the way our human suffering not only humbles us, but also fuels us. The statement about power being made perfect in weakness is especially profound, given our understanding of the soul's journey.

We need our weaknesses in order to discover our strengths. When we are in the midst of a dark night of the soul, we become very aware of our weaknesses. It is typically a period when our self-esteem and confidence are at an all-time low. But the goal is not to do away with our weaknesses completely, but rather, to look for God's grace in the midst of it. Sometimes it is the reflection on our weaknesses which motivates a new career or life direction. You may decide to become a wounded healer, for example. In that way, you alchemize the wound into a gift that can guide others. We can't plead our wounds and weaknesses away, but we can allow them to make us whole. We can grant them the ability to give us strength, and we can use that strength to make a difference in the world. That is the lesson of Paul's thorn.

Finally, a similar theme comes to the surface when you explore the story of Christ. On the one hand, the story of Jesus is tragic. Bursting with compassion and under-standing, Jesus made it his sole mission to spread love and lead by example. He healed through love and inspired a nation through preaching his God-given wisdom. But in the end, he was crucified for his pursuits. He was forced to suffer and even die, by the very people he was trying to save. But following his death, he was resurrected, which reveals something about the human soul. Sometimes a part of us needs to die in order to live out our mission with renewed power. Without Christ's resurrection, there would be no glory. This reveals something about our personal crosses that we all must bear. If your ego-self does not die, there is no space for a metamorphosis. And without metamorphosis, there is no growth. No evolution. Ortlund (2021).

It can be difficult to stay in tune with our divine natures when everything is going right, or according to plan. It's easy to take things for granted, or lose sight of the truth at these junctures. But when the chips are low, our ego's are ripe for moulding. It's easier to surrender to a higher purpose because all of our previous attachments are lost or given new meaning. This can provide comfort if you are in the middle of your own dark night of the soul. Suffering serves a purpose, and it acts as the necessary precursor to life's bounty and gold. Jesus knew this. Paul knew this. And many others learned through the process of their own dark nights. So long as you can find the grace amidst the struggle, you'll emerge anew. You'll have more strength and more certainty than ever before.

The list is infinite. The amount of people who have suffered greatly and gone on to do even greater things in life and for others is endless.

What is your gift in the darkness?

Chapter 8

Dark Night of the Soul vs. Depression

There can be no rebirth without a dark night of the soul, a total annihilation of all that you believed in and thought that you were.

– Hazrat Inayat Khan

———— ··●·· ————

The "dark night of the soul" is a specific brand of deep suffering. It is a concept that goes back hundreds of years in history. In the 16th century, poet and mystic Saint John of the Cross wrote about the dark night of the soul in La Noche Oscura Del Alma, and wrestled to discern between depression and a dark night of the soul. The symptoms are similar, but you will feel the difference in the depth of spiritual transformation that occurs.

The deep suffering associated with a dark night of the soul is known by other terms in other disciplines. In Shamanism, this prolonged state is called "soul loss" or descent to the underworld. In Greek mythology, it is known as katabasis, and Carl Jung understood it symbolically in terms of alchemy as nigredo. Each reference is about a period of darkness where your soul is separated from God. During this split, your false self is wholly destroyed, and you are remade into your true self.

Most people who experience a dark night of the soul realize that nothing makes them happy anymore. They can no longer experience bodily or sexual pleasure, their emotions are dulled, and no joy comes from material possessions or even spiritual practice. This state of intense apathy is the beginning of the purification process, and it is another blessing in disguise.

This is easy enough to theorize about, but when you are going through it in reality, it is absolutely terrifying. The ground beneath your feet is ripped out from beneath you, and you are in the midst of great loss and suffering. Such are the trials of life. When it's happening, all you want is for it to stop. You do not immediately recognize that your suffering is a positive omen of change. It does not feel like that, but it is there to let you know that you can no longer continue to live the way you have been living.

We have been discussing the two things side by side all along without calling attention to the difference between suffering and a dark night of the soul, and the two experiences do have important differences between them.

Not all suffering is as intense as a dark night. Not all suffering is about resolving imbalanced karmic energy. Sometimes, you just suffer hardship, and it's terrible, and you get through it, and not much else has changed.

With a dark night of the soul, though, life is very intense for an extended time. Your core center is deeply unsatisfied as your whole being lives the experience of resolving karma. People move in and out of your life swiftly and with divine purpose and timing. Your soul is on the move as you suffer, as you are becoming a seeker of knowledge and spiritual wisdom. Burning desires grip you desperately and do not let you go. They remain there, burning inside of you until you resolve the obstacles and surrounding tension that has suffocated your desires for too long.

Not only are you on fire from the inside, but things burn away from the outside world as well when undergoing a dark night of the soul. More than suffering a "bad day" or a "tough time" as you normally would, the spiritual casing that wraps the darkness also flavors this brand of suffering quite differently. You will lose complete interest in physical things, your mind will travel down complicated rabbit holes of discovery where you find there is so much more to learn.

The more you learn, the more you grow and evolve, the more your intuition comes online and your communication channels open, the more your spirit awakens. When you are finally through it, you are not the same person you were when it began.

When you suffer, in general, you might reach a point of anger with God, but this fury is not attached to your suffering. With a dark night of the soul, you are at war with God, demanding an end to your pain. In the beginning, you latch yourself onto a cycle of anger. You're angry with God, then you're angry with yourself, then you're angry at life. It just keeps going until you realize what is happening. Then, depending upon your purpose and where your soul is in its evolution, the darkness lasts until it clears.

As with any period of suffering, there is no good answer to the question of how long this will last. Take comfort in knowing your soul has a higher purpose, —otherwise, you would not suffer this way. Take comfort in also knowing that you will be led to and through every node of growth along the way so that you are given a salve as you go through the suffering.

Some have defined this as a time of spiritual despair. You feel disconnected and empty. The emptiness is from feeling completely divided from God. It is a time of sadness, loss, and spiritual urgency. The darkness of the night is when your eyes are closed and you must rely on other senses. Not only do you lose connection with God and feel devoid of all spirituality, but you feel betrayed by life itself and find yourself without a sure ground to walk upon. In the darkness of the night, your old life loses its meaning and falls away so that you can grow into a new version of yourself.

The term is misleading as it lasts much longer than a night. Just how long your suffering will last is unpredictable, but some have likened the terminology to what's known as a "polar night". This phenomenon occurs at the northernmost and southernmost poles of the Earth. Because of the tilt of the Earth's axis, the area inside these polar circles experiences a 'night' that lasts longer than

24 hours. As awful as the prolonged darkness seems, it holds astonishing potential because the opposite can also occur. The "polar day" happens when the sun is above the horizon for longer than 24 hours in the same areas of the Earth but at a different point in time. It makes sense to conceptualize 'day' and 'night' here as abstract and undefined seasons of time similar to your soul's suffering and the lasting fulfillment that comes with your freedom from suffering.

Many people liken this experience to the clinical diagnosis of depression. Conventionally, this is how people speak of their suffering: in terms of being depressed. In this state of impaired mental health, you feel there is no purpose to anything, and nothing makes sense anymore. However, a dark night of the soul is a state of total impairment of health. This variety of suffering impacts your physical, mental, emotional, and spiritual health. The depression that you feel is real. It is part of your suffering, but it is not the totality of your suffering. You will feel what people with depression feel. You may want to withdraw from the world or remove yourself from it. These feelings are normal.

One important difference between depression and a dark night of the soul is that depression can be treated with medication and therapy to the point of alleviating some or all of the mental health suffering. In short, you treat the two things differently. Depression is a likely part of your dark night of the soul, but not everyone who is depressed is going through one. The source of depression is also different from the source of suffering during a dark night of the soul. Depression is rooted in chemical imbalances in the body and self-sabotaging thought patterns and can result from illness, abuse, or genetics. In comparison, a dark night is rooted in your soul's existential crisis and can result from simply embarking upon your soul's journey.

Some sure signs will alert you to the fact that you're going through a dark night of the soul rather than suffering from depression alone. If you can check all or most of these boxes, it might help you accept where you are on your soul's journey. Keep in mind that these are also symptoms of depression, so by themselves they are not enough to differentiate between the two states of suffering. It's helpful to think of them as depression and dark night depression.

The first is a heavy feeling of sadness. It doesn't matter why you are in despair or what caused it, it only matters that you feel unhappy. The next clue is that on top of the sadness, you also feel unworthy. You are sure you do not deserve the happiness you lost, nor do you deserve anything remotely positive to enter your sphere. You don't deserve love, respect, success, attention, or to feel better.

The persistent feeling of being doomed to a life of suffering is another sign of a dark night. The emptiness will feel eternal. In truth, all of the symptoms might feel eternal. Another dark night marker is feeling powerless to change your situation and hopeless that it will improve. Compound that with the fact that your self-control will be compromised, and it will be hard for you to take any kind of action. This is not to say that you can't or won't take action, but it will be difficult. It will also be challenging to find joy in the things you once loved or even the energy or drive to do them. The general feeling of craving will also persist, and you will long for comfort, but the comfort of your known world will be gone.

Taken together, these symptoms of depression synthesize into a dark night depression that is more philosophical than the usual melancholia. Another key distinction between depression and a dark night of the soul is how the two brands of suffering end. When you come out of your depression, you are pretty much the same person you were: You still have your usual habits, thought patterns, and beliefs, and the only real difference is that you feel better—thankfully!

When your dark night of the soul ends (and it will end eventually), your former life is unrecognizable. Little remains the same. Not only do you feel better and recategorize your life as an incredible experience, but you think better, relate better, and connect with God better.

Chapter 9

The Dark Night of the Soul Journey & What to Expect

If God sends us on strong paths, we are pro-
vided strong shoes. – Corrie ten Boom

— ··●·· —

There are several inevitabilities on the journey through the dark night of the soul. For one, life gets very intense. Usually, there is some form of loss or separation, which serves as the catalyst for resolving karma. When all of your ego structures fall and shatter, there's no choice but to build yourself back again. It's a painful, and often grueling process, but it's also the means toward greater clarity and authenticity. It offers the path toward true fulfilment. But the process of loss and re-identification is intense. It often feels like a sort of death, like you're forced to start at ground zero once more. The core of who you are will feel profoundly unsatisfied and people may come and go as you learn who you are all over again. Life may slow down at first, but then pick up speed soon afterward as your soul rushes to move around and achieve progress. You will suddenly become a seeker on a quest for spiritual truths. And through that quest, you will discover parts of yourself you didn't know existed. This is where the healing begins...

Through the process of rediscovery, you'll find that many beliefs you once held were actually rooted in fears, traumas, and internalized false negatives. For example, the dark night of the soul usually heralds an epiphany, in which a person realizes that a certain self-belief is not actually their belief, but rather their family's, friend's, or partner's. When I experienced my own dark night of the soul, I was very critical of myself. After the failure of a codependent relationship, I thought there was something wrong with me. I thought that I wasn't successful enough because my parents never told me they were proud of me. I thought that I was too sensitive because I was never allowed to show emotion as a child--feelings were swept under the rug in my home, never to be discussed. All of this created a false narrative within me. For years, I held on to the belief that I was somehow inferior. On a conscious level, I thought that I deserved things like love, success and happiness. But on a subconscious level, some part of me felt that I wasn't worthy.

When my relationship ended and my best friends moved to a different state for grad school, I was all alone. So, I had to redefine myself and learn how to be self-sufficient. It was no longer acceptable for me to seek happiness through external sources such as other people or personal achievements. I needed to find it from within. This was difficult, because I had never done it before, but I knew there was a reason for this. I knew that through the tunnel of struggle, I would find a light that didn't flicker or wane...a permanent glow. So instead of following my friends to a new state, I got my own apartment and began the difficult process of building a new life. That's when I discovered my true vocation of healing and life-coaching. It's also when I met the love of my life.

The whole experience was terrifying. I was in the unknown, lonely and afraid. But through building something from square one, I learned that many of the beliefs about myself I had held from childhood, were actually false. Through meeting a partner who appreciated my sensitivities, I learned that I wasn't too sensitive. Through discovering my passion for healing, I learned that I wasn't a failure by society's standards, I just simply hadn't found my niche. And through falling in love again and making myself vulnerable, I learned that I was worthy of happiness and abundance. There wasn't anything wrong with me. I was simply wrong for holding onto negative beliefs. Now, I am forever changed. I'll never be the person I was before my dark night of the soul. Now, I live through my soul's purpose and find endless energy and motivation through its life-giving sustenance. My life is very different, but it also has new meaning. It's different in a good way. The experience left me whole and healed.

These are the things you can expect to experience during your own dark night of the soul. As you lose grip on the things that previously framed your ego identity, you will find new burning desires within you. You will find a new spiritual appreciation for life and the voice of your intuition will gain volume as you can't help but hear and respond to its nudges. Once you hear the whispers from your intuition and you begin the process of reorienting your life based on those nudges, you are ready to walk into the light. It's impossible to say how long your journey with the dark night of the soul will take. For some people, it may last a few months. For others, it may last several years. More likely than not, it will arrive as a gradual process. One significant change may set the whole process in motion, but the struggles and resulting revelations could crop up for several years in sudden bursts.

The length of your dark night may also depend on your specific purpose. If your true purpose requires more tests and challenges to build you up, then your path through the darkness may be longer, but the light at the end of the tunnel will be richer and brighter as well. Some of us require more struggle to get to our final destination, and that's okay. Remember, your soul chose your path for a reason. Deep down, you know that you must endure and that you will survive. In fact, you'll not only survive, but thrive in a new form. Additionally, depending on how evolved your soul is in your current incarnation, you may not need a lengthy dark night. If you're already fairly evolved on a soul level, you may be able to pick up the pieces of your life and listen to your intuition when it first makes its presence known. After that, you can work toward making your life what you want it to be, and the darkness will dissipate with each step toward progress.

Sometimes, the length of your dark night journey is dependent upon other puzzle pieces that are waiting to fall into place. Maybe you're meant to meet a soulmate or some other significant guide, but so long as you hesitate to go out into the world, your progress is stunted. Sometimes your soul must wait for another soul to meet you on your path. And this will no doubt affect the timing of your own dark night. Remember that your soul cluster is like an intricate web. It relies on precise timing to offer fated encounters that may change the course of your life. And sometimes, your dark night may include bursts of light. You may meet your soulmate while you're still working on finding your purpose. This helps to lessen the anxiety of the whole experience. Just because a dark night of the soul is dark, doesn't mean that it has to be entirely painful. We all experience difficult months or years, but within those periods, we also have moments of hope, amusement, or light. So even if your dark night ends up lasting longer than the average person's, it's not all bad. You may just need more time to access the abundance of light within you.

In extreme cases, you may experience harsh lows during your dark night cycle. These are all extremes, but some people endure difficult situation such as suicidal thoughts, a lack of inner peace, dullness in life, or a period of extreme introversion. As previously mentioned, some people lose their friends, parents, or spouses. Sometimes, people have sleepless nights and find that their mental, emotional or physical health is damaged. Other times, a new physical ailment arises that leads to feelings of insecurity. You may lose your faith in God or any form of a higher power. And all of this could lead to anger directed at yourself or your life. While each of these situations are difficult and even traumatizing, it's important to remember that there is a deeper meaning and purpose to such events. Sometimes it's our greatest suffering which produces our greatest gifts. Through that awareness, you can embrace difficult periods as a lesson and a means toward evolved growth. Suffering brings growth, a chance for healing and a creative opportunity to discover personal strength. If you fall into one of these extreme cases, don't worry. There is always a light at the end of the tunnel. Remember that the dark night of the soul is a rite of passage, and you will come out the other side, healed and metamorphosed.

The dark night of the soul can be broken down into seven specific stages. First, there is the moment when you wake up to the truth. This falls closely in line with a triggering event, or maybe even several triggering events. Then, comes the fall to rock bottom--the period of loss and decay. Next, is the chaos of major ups and downs, followed by a renewed sense of purpose. Then, with a new sense of balance and stability, you have the ability to transform into the very best version of yourself. This is generally the timeline for the dark night of the soul, and each and every step is an important milestone toward meaning and wholeness. You can't skip on in order to fast-forward to the next. Each step serves a purpose that provides wisdom and truth. So, let's explore each of these steps more thoroughly...

It's no surprise that the first inciting incident on the dark night journey involves a waking up to the truth. You suddenly realize that the old things you attributed so much meaning to no longer feel very meaningful. It's like a punch in your gut which indicates, 'I need a new source of meaning.' Life becomes dull and purposeless. This sensation may arrive at the onset of loss, or it may take some time before it settles in. But once the feeling arrives, there is no denying it. It's an emptiness that begs the soul to transform and shape shift. Once you accept the truth that life needs new meaning, that your ego must die and be reborn again, then you're ready to accept the dark night of the soul as your essential rite of passage. You can begin the critical journey.

Afterward, you may experience a triggering event or, perhaps, multiple triggering events which further illuminate the need for greater meaning. The context and substance of these events will differ for every person, but generally they bring loss of some form. You may lose your job after losing a partner or loved one. Your friends may move away or a parent may pass away. There are a wide variety of events which may trigger the stereotypical dark night depression. However, these events are heralding something new. They're meant to shake the foundation of your life so new flowers can emerge through the cracks. In order to gain, we also have to sacrifice. So, while you may feel like the world is delivering a cruel and dark fate, this is just an essential turning point. The universe is decluttering so you have room for something new. It may feel tragic because the dark night of the soul usually promises several difficult events. There may be the initial event which wakes you up to the truth, but the following event plummets you into the next phase...the darkness of the underworld.

The darkest time arrives at the third stage of the soul's progression. This is because all of the major incidents have already occurred, and you have time and space to mourn but also reflect on what's missing. Through grieving whatever has slipped away, you realize what matters most to you. If you lost a significant partner, for example, you need time to mourn the relationship and identify why it mattered to you so much. Once you've fully allowed yourself to experience the emotions, and feel the weight of the loss, you can begin the process of healing and looking forward. You can look to the future with curiosity and see that in the midst of all the chaos, there is also excitement. The universe is preparing you for something. Anything can happen at any moment, and while depression may still linger, there is also hope and a sense of openness.

After hitting "rock bottom," there is usually a sort of rollercoaster effect. You may experience moments of pure bliss and joy, followed by prolonged phases of stress, anxiety or depression. You may have good days followed by bad days as you try to navigate what makes you happy while you're on empty. This is a difficult period, but a necessary one, nonetheless. You need this time to feel the highs and lows before you're ready to discover a deeper meaning. Before we can devote ourselves to something, we need to feel what it means to be truly alive. Sometimes, being alive is a chaotic experience. This period of time can make it feel as though you're going crazy. You may be jumping for joy one minute, and crying the next. But these are the kinds of experiences you need to achieve balance and stability once more. It's like the pendulum which swings back and forth before landing in the center. You need to give yourself time to live after feeling the effects of rock bottom. Boomer (2020).

After you've given yourself time and space to live and experience every emotion, you're nearly ready to discover your purpose. This is when a new sense of meaning kicks in. You've overcome the darkest of lows and you've endured the resulting rollercoaster transition. Now, you're ready to feel grounded and powerful. There's a curious sensation that occurs after you've gone through something difficult. After you make your way through the bleakness of the tunnel, a new sense of confidence awaits. You have an understanding that you've dealt with difficult things and you survived. Other things that may have seemed scary before, no longer seem so terrifying. You understand that you can do difficult things and even come out stronger on the other side. This is how you set the stage for new meaning.

With the inner peace that comes from knowing your past was a significant milestone, you can carry forward with acceptance and even gratitude. You know that all of the pain you endured served a higher purpose. It's at that moment, that your unique purpose finds voice. You may discover that you have more compassion for yourself and for the rest of humanity than you previously understood. This could lead to the pursuit of a career in a helping field. Through becoming more spiritually focused, you may seek work that includes a higher spiritual purpose.

However, that's not the only kind of purpose that is revealed. Some people cultivate different kinds of strength during their dark night of the soul. For example, someone may have a friend who is overly critical. Maybe this friend has made them feel bad about a certain talent because they're jealous. The dark night of the soul may very well end the friendship, which could be devastating but also eye-opening. With the friendship behind them, they discover their talent once more with an internal strength that's ever enduring. They no longer question their abilities because they know that one person can't decide their worth. This is just one example of how a dark night of the soul leads to a clearer sense of purpose.

Additionally, you may decide to pursue something completely different after your passage through the dark tunnel. You may have an experience or a moment of sudden insight which reveals an unknown skill or desire. It is not uncommon for people to totally change paths after a dark night of the soul. It is a transformation, afterall. This is especially common if you've been putting all your attention into one area of life while neglecting something else. For example, maybe you spent the first twenty-eight years of your life focused on making money. You may have taken a job that is similar to your parents which promised financial security, but after a few years you realize that it doesn't make you feel passionate. Maybe the money earned you a nice home with nice things, but upon having all those nice things, an emptiness still lingers. This is a sign that it's time to listen to your soul and pursue something entirely different. These are the common experiences that occur during a dark night of the soul.

Everyone has a different experience with the dark night of the soul. No two experiences look identical, but there are certainly commonalities which are expected across the board. You'll no doubt encounter a feeling of emptiness, and some form of external loss. You'll definitely feel some combination of confusion and shock as your old life fractures to create room for new experiences. Once the emptiness sinks in and it's fully processed, you'll find increased motivation, passion and energy. Through overcoming a period of depression, you'll awaken to a new sense of who you are and what you're meant to accomplish with your life. These outcomes are true of every dark night of the soul. So, although the inevitable darkness is scary, the inevitable light at the end of the tunnel is equally rewarding. Your dark night won't last forever, so continue being strong and showing up for yourself.

Someday someone will break you so badly that you'll become unbreakable – Joker (Batman Movie)

Chapter 10

Healing Yourself

The soul usually knows what to do to heal itself. The challenge is to silence the mind. — Caroline Myss

— ··•·· —

H ealing is tricky. It begins when you're down, depressed, and have a lot of emotional processing to do, but it doesn't flourish in this state. You become aware of the need to heal, and you start to question your mind's role in the process. When you're deep in your suffering, the first thing you have to learn is how to grab hold of your mind and reprogram it piece by piece. Until you do, it will run its default programming—which is part of what got you into so much suffering to begin with.

The good news is that once you see how you have been subconsciously sabotaging yourself and your efforts, you realize that you can turn it around and use the same cognitive machinery in your favor. Everything that feels like it is happening to you, remember, is happening for you. It is all happening to open you up to God and your higher self. Don't fight it so hard, for resistance only causes greater pain.

A good spiritual principle here is to remember that what you resist persists. As soon as humanly possible, surrender your soul's journey over to the divine source of energy that pushes all willing beings toward their fullest potential.

Most of us suffer from some form of childhood trauma, either on a micro or macro level. Our parents may have loved us, but not in the way that we needed them to. Or maybe we were bullied in school. Sometimes a seemingly mild event can have psychological repercussions that last and linger for decades. The healing process serves to eradicate these traumas which have been affecting our mental health covertly, under the surface. The healing process them to light so that we can all live brighter lives. Healing is the final gift. It's the light at the end of the tunnel. When suffering has come and gone, we find ourselves stronger, happier, and healthier than ever before.

The dark night of the soul can feel very negative and even hopeless. It's a period when many of your attachments slip away, leaving you empty and afraid. However, if you focus on the healing that the dark night promises. You can engage with the process with curiosity, rather than fear. Through focusing on the healing, you keep your attention on the light instead of the dark. This will help to carry you through. But, of course, it's easier said than done. You may be wondering how, exactly, one focuses on healing when it feels like life is slipping through your fingers. It may seem like a fruitless effort but there are absolutely certain things you can do to lessen anxiety and stay focused on the healing.

Let's discuss what can we do to help ourselves. There are to-do's, not-to-do's and effective and simple healing techniques.

What Not to do:

Don't ignore your issue - Some people are experts at hiding their depression. They would rather bury their emotions than face them. For many of us, this is the more desirable option, because facing depression requires work.

Depressive emotions are painful. It isn't fun to sit with negativity, but the negativity provides creative options. If you sit with the pain long enough, you'll discover new insights along with newfound motivation. Through releasing the emotions, you can cleanse your system and course correct. But you can't rush this process and you can't ignore it either. The only way past the darkness is through it. So don't ignore or repress the fact that you're depressed. Acknowledge the pain and get curious about it. You'll discover that you have more strength and power than you ever previously imagined.

Don't drink to excess - Many people turn to drugs and alcohol when they're depressed because substances act as an escape. Through numbing the pain, depressed people attempt to cope through a quick fix. However, quick fixes don't do anything to heal the core issue. Excessive drinking can result in a whole new set of problems. It can tear families apart, destroy the body and the liver, and wreak havoc in a number of ways. So, avoid creating new problems for yourself through the excessive use of substances. Instead, sit with the pain and find healthy ways to care for yourself.

Don't let your sleeping schedule get out of control - Sleep is so important when you're depressed. Because your mind is suffering, your body needs to be in top form. Through allowing yourself the sleep you need; you're telling yourself that you care about your body. Sleep nurtures your entire system. When you're depressed, however, it's easy to experience restless nights. Your mind may be racing and you may have trouble relaxing. If this is the case, do whatever you can to make sure your body gets the rest it needs.

Don't lock yourself indoors -It's easy to become a recluse when you feel depressed. Socializing can seem exhausting and far too overstimulating for your sensitive state. However, it's important that you don't lock yourself indoors because socializing is often the thing that has the power to energize you. Humans thrive on connection. They need to be out in the world, interacting with others in order to feel satisfied. Additionally, exploring the great outdoors is a healthy practice. We feel lighter when we're out in nature. We feel more grounded and more connected to the larger universe around us. So, resist the urge to lock yourself indoors when sadness takes over. Go explore the world. Even if you only have enough energy for a short walk outside, make yourself walk! You'll be thankful you did.

Don't escape too much into video games or other virtual distractions - The world has never been more saturated with distractions. Whether it's our phones, our apps, social media, television, or the news, distractions are all around us at all hours of the day. When we're depressed, it's easy to lean into the distractions. Depression eradicates passion. It also depletes us of our energy. So, it makes sense that we would attempt to fill our voids with television and excessive internet use. This is not advised, however, because these distractions are just another quick fix. They don't help the healing process. Escaping into the world of video games could prove healing at first. It may momentarily distract you from your pain. But you can't play video games forever, and if you try to, you will start to feel foggy and lifeless. Use your distractions when you need a distraction. But don't rely on these things like a crutch. The only way past depression is through it. Quick fixes do not address the core issue.

Resist the urge to wallow in sad music - It's important to embrace negative emotions, but it's also important to detach when necessary. Sadness needs to be felt and released, but there's a difference between releasing emotions and wallowing in them. Some people, when depressed, prefer to sit with the sadness and let it consume them. This can lead to feelings of being sorry for oneself. At worst, it results in a sort of pity party. Again, it is productive to sit with emotions, but once you've released everything you can, it's important to get up and move on. Don't get in the habit of wallowing. Let the release act as a source of energy and motivation. Brush yourself off, get back up again, and go experience the world.

Avoid comparing yourself to other people - Comparison is a nasty habit, and yet we're all prone to practicing it. It's easy to look at someone else and think, 'They have it together...why don't I?' Maybe these people appear put together on the outside, with many accomplishments and successes. However, it's impossible to fully understand the experience of another human being. Everyone has their struggles, no matter how polished they may seem on the outside. So, it's often inaccurate to assume someone is in a better position than you are. Comparison is unproductive because at the end of the day, you're only competing with yourself. So, avoid the habit of comparing yourself to others. Instead, reflect on your own life and the things you want. Then, consider the practical steps you can take to make those wants a new reality.

Don't feel guilty about depression - If you're someone who's typically upbeat and social, you may feel guilty about your depressed feelings. You may want to mask your emotions around other people and put on a "happy face." If you tend to be a people-pleaser, this is especially true. But the truth is, everyone experiences bouts of depression, and it's not something to feel guilty about. It's okay to own the fact that you're depressed. Depression is a means toward growth. It serves a purpose in our lives as humans. So don't be ashamed of it. It's an essential rite of passage, and you're a human being just like everyone else. If you have to deny invitations or take moments to yourself at social gatherings, don't be afraid to do so. You must do whatever you can to manage your depression effectively, and that includes owning it and taking responsibility for it.

Don't think too hard about the future - When we're depressed, we tend to overanalyze future possibilities because it gives us hope for a better future. At the same time, though, this can be a defense mechanism because we want to control the future. When we're in stressed or chaotic states, the urge to control life grows even stronger. But unfortunately, we're never able to control our destinies. Therefore, we have no choice but to limit the amount of time we spend hypothesizing about the future. Life happens in the present, and reflecting on the future may feel good at times, but in the end, it's not very productive. Think about what you want your future to look like, and make plans to achieve that. But avoid ruminating on future possibilities. If you spend too much time trying to figure out what's going to happen next, you're only going to make yourself fearful and exhausted. It's a waste of time to put too much weight on things we can't control.

Think carefully about embarking on a new relationship - Relationships are obviously a source of joy and healing, but some relationships also have the power to sabotage our progress. If your depression was catalyzed by the end of a serious or romantic relationship, you should consider pausing before jumping into a new romantic relationship. Sometimes it's hard to know ourselves if we're constantly living for others. Relationships always require sacrifice. And depression usually calls for some selfishness. So, although it's natural to crave new relationships when you're down, you should be honest with yourself and consider the various reasons why you're craving those relationships. What does romance give you that you can't give yourself? What are some other ways you can fill your personal voids? The stronger you are as an independent person, the stronger your relationships will be because you'll be a whole person who knows and understands yourself.

Don't suffer alone - It's easy to withdraw when we're depressed. Our first instinct may be to spend lots of time alone in our rooms. There's still a nasty stigma around depression, which leads people to isolate and shut themselves off from the rest of the world. Some people believe that there is strength in suffering alone, but this is false. When we allow ourselves to be vulnerable, when we share our feelings and allow others to support us, we lessen our own loads and find healing through connection. It may seem scary, but you'd be surprised just how much others are willing and eager to help when you show vulnerability. Humans have a natural desire to help each other. And it's often through sharing in our pain, that we achieve the highest level of healing. So, if your inclination is to suffer alone, try calling a friend instead. Hire a therapist, or phone a family member. These simple acts can do wonders when it comes to accessing strength and inner peace. Through letting others in, we learn that we are not alone in our experiences. Misery loves company afterall.

What to do:

Journaling - You could try journaling during this time to strengthen your connection with yourself. This is how you open up your communication channels. First, you tap into your inner narrative. Write out the contents of your mind. Starting is the hardest part. Once you get going, your subconscious will begin to empty onto the page. Begin anywhere. Begin by writing your dreams or visions. Begin by writing your daily routine. Begin wherever you want as long as you start somewhere.

A journal is also a good place to practice gratitude, which is of the highest vibrational energy in the universe. Be grateful for everything, and write it down. Write down everything you are grateful for, even the small things that seem insignificant. Say thank you for all of it—the good and the bad, the positive and the negative, the dark and the light.

Write down your prayers, write down your goals, write down the dreams that come to you at night, and spend some time with them. Spend some time with yourself in words, and you will open up your communication quickly. Once you are in connection with yourself, you can begin to open the space between you and your higher self. This will pull in more energy that feeds your budding intuition and self-awareness.

Focus on yourself first - Keep the focus on yourself during this dark time. You're in no shape to take on the suffering or problems of others, for you have plenty of your own to deal with. This is not the time to debate your selfishness versus your selflessness. This is the time for your soul to evolve—and you need all of your energy for this!

Find your Support - Find a new support network. Most likely, you will lose some if not all of your usual support, and you will have to look outside of your known social circles for new friends, coaches, and well-wishers. It is of the utmost importance that you do this, that you seek out, find, and accept support in your life. The people who enter your sphere may not be who you expect or even want, but they are there for a reason. The same goes for those who must exit your sphere. Let them go, as it is time for your soul's journey to part from theirs. It does not mean that you will never see them again, although sometimes this is what happens. It just means it's time to part ways with some and walk in stride with others.

If it resonates with you, seek out a spiritual teacher for yourself. A guru or enlightened being with a higher perspective is very helpful if you can find one—or if one finds you.

Music and Dance - There was a period of time in my life where Music and Dance was my only friend. I forced myself out to go out social dancing. I enrolled for social dance classes. Being in the company of other people and in an environment of Music helped me to temporarily forget the trauma in the mind. This helped mind to recover.

Seek these avenues out. Find ways to incorporate music into your day and life, specifically ways that force you to produce music and rhythm with your body. This is an excellent way to release the stored, blocked emotions that have been dormant in you for years but that now are bubbling up to the surface to be released. Release them. Shake them out of you. The music helps. Plus, you avoid doing further damage to your health.

Engage in social activities - Other people are helpful, too, in a different way. Even though it will present challenges, find social gatherings to attend. If the opportunity arises for you to be social, or at least among others, take it. If you are invited to do something, say yes. Loneliness will only escalate depression and suffering, so take care to alleviate it by being near people when you can. It doesn't have to be a party; any gathering will do. You could even combine it with music and find a class, group, or event that offers music and the company of others. This will divert your attention from the physical, mental, emotional, and spiritual suffering you are in the midst of.

Do what your love - During this time, if something brings you an ounce of joy, take it. Listen to your intuition and your heart and find the activities that speak to you and that you love. When you find them, keep them, and work them into your routine.

As you suffer, shed, molt, and transform, it is important to take in the joyous feelings, or at least the feelings of calm or neutrality. Allow these energies to fill the space that was once occupied by your former self.

Meditation - The depression that accompanies your soul's suffering can be eased if you take proper care. Psychotherapy, talk therapy, medication, and support groups are good for your mental health. Exercise, yoga, dance, walking, and many other movements also help improve your well-being. Mindfulness and faith practices are all

welcome alleviations of depression. Meditation, especially, helps tame the distractions and illusions of the mind.
There are many forms of meditation, so find the one that
suits you best. Almost anything can be adapted to a meditative practice, even doing the dishes.

The point is that you need to relax. This will allow you
to be open and surrender to the process. You need to find
a way to release the pressure that has built up from trying
to figure everything out and tirelessly thinking yourself
into circles. You're burnt out because your mind is on full
throttle all of the time, and you need to stop that mental track and begin to watchfully observe your thought
patterns and reactions to fully enter the space of transformation. Make relaxation a priority to avoid feelings of
hopelessness, dread, and overwhelm.

You may also consider guided meditations. These are
great for beginners who want to meditate but feel intim-
idated or anxious that they may be doing it incorrectly. If
that's the case, you can simply find a guided meditation
on YouTube, Spotify, or any number of other streaming
services. You can also receive a guided meditation from a
person in real life. Additionally, you can choose a specific form of guided meditations based on the specific issues you may want to address. There is a wide array of
issues which guided meditations cover, including addic-

tions, low self-esteem, anger, anxiety, emotional management, pain management, loss of creativity, and so much
more.

Take care of your health - Take conscious action in favor
of your health. You don't need to be the hero who slays
the beast and fights to obliterate the darkness; that's not
what this journey is about. What you need to do is put
yourself first and muster all of the strength of heart you
can embody.

Be of service - A sure way to feel healing work in your life
is to serve others. When you begin to serve the world, the
darkness that surrounds you will change. Opening your
heart to serve others will not make the darkness disap-
pear—nor should it—but it will bring light into your life.

Be patient - Be patient with yourself. This is one of the
greatest virtues.

Healing is a gradual process. Just as you suffer on all
levels of being, you also heal on all levels of being. You heal
your body along with your mind, emotions, relationships,
and spirit. It takes time. The more you know and are aware
of what you're going through and why, the better understanding you have of the bigger processes involved. You
are not alone. This is often the first step of finding new
meaning to hold onto again after so much suffering. Once
that small amount of purpose returns, it gives new hope

and positively affects the frustration and sadness you feel, leaving you with a sense of ease. It's like cracking a window for fresh air to circulate into a stale room, or opening the door to a dark room just enough for a ray of light to seep in.

Awareness - Close your eyes, and focus on your breath. Through focusing on your breath, and eliminating all of your outside thoughts, you practice staying in the moment. When you do that enough times, your brain reorients itself. This looks easy, but it takes lot of practice to quiet the monkey mind.

It also helps you to observe your thoughts and feelings from a distance. Awareness puts you in a detached state where you're operating from the subconscious, rather than conscious reality. For this reason, you can observe your feelings from the outside and learn how to experience them without feeling overwhelmed by them. Overall, awareness does wonders for facilitating a more peaceful and freeing life existence.

Dreams and Visions - Dreams are a window to your soul. I have a book and pen beside my pillow and scribble in my lucid dreaming state. In the morning I review what I had scribbled in the night and journal them in proper diary. Have done this for many years. I have developed very good intuition during this process. The more you trust your inner self, the more gets revealed to you. I have become very good at analyzing not only my dreams but also my family and extended family members dreams.

Due to the nature of my trainings in the night in the higher levels of consciousness, most of my dreams were revealing dark hidden fears in my subconscious mind (like snakes, fearsome animals, dark forest, travelling alone and afraid). Also, in many cases the Dreams were prophecies of plans for Humanity, Earth and Universe.

Be open to change - It's equally important to stay open in a general sense. As difficult as it may be, try to avoid fighting or resisting the chaos that the dark night of the soul brings. The root of struggle is resistance. So rather than resist, try to embrace the changes that are occurring with curiosity and wonder. Remember that the dark night of the soul is a necessary metamorphosis. Transformation is a natural part of life. If you try to fight the transformation, it will only persist with greater force. So instead, open yourself up and try to float with the changes of the wind. If you lead with the knowledge that life is supporting you, that your soul knows where it needs to go even if your consciousness is still in the dark, you will have a much easier time embracing the changes that occur. All of the hardships and challenges serve a deeper purpose. Life is leading you toward a road to greater fulfilment. So don't resist the process. The process is your coming home.

When you stop fighting, you allow yourself to be over-taken by the forces at work in your life. Some people talk about surrender as if it means giving yourself over to your enemy, but this is not the case with surrendering to the darkness of suffering in your soul. In this instance, surrender is about ending your resistance, accepting your soul's journey, and letting things happen. When you surrender, you put your trust in the universe and the process

One of the game-changing perspective shifts we can make on the path of evolutionary awakening is learning to befriend the discomfort that comes with change. If we can start to see this discomfort as something positive and realize that it's a result of the fact that we're growing, it changes everything.

This is, of course, easier said than done. Let's face it: we human beings are animals and we relate to discomfort as a negative thing. It's part of how we're wired. We're deeply conditioned to believe that feeling bad is bad, and feeling good is good. It's one of the most primary orientations to life that all of us have. And this makes sense. Who wants to feel bad? We all want to feel good. It's natural. But it's also natural that a lot of the good things in life—growth, development, and evolution—also come with some degree of feeling bad.

If we want to evolve, we need to shift our perspective so that we can start to see this discomfort more as the natural growing pains that accompany any kind of positive change.

Surrender to the process - Saint Faustina, of the Divine Mercy Devotion, often wrote about the importance of surrendering to suffering. She said, "Oh, if only the suffering soul knew how it is loved by God, it would die of joy and excess of happiness! Someday, we will know the value of suffering, but then we will no longer be able to suffer. The present moment is ours."

In response, the Lord says to Saint Faustina, "My daughter, suffering will be a sign to you that I am with you."

Saint Faustina's sentiment implies that the hereafter is the only place where you can awaken to the gifts of suffering, but it also champions the present moment as our time to claim. You can know the value of suffering now, in the present moment. That intelligence is available to you and will help you through the very suffering it entails.

Warrior mindset - You need to develop a warrior's mindset with a single-minded focus. Meditation, hypnosis, support, therapy, and spirituality are all useful weapons to have in your healing arsenal. To specifically target your subconscious mind and reprogram it, you might choose to focus on affirmations or mantras. Repeated sounds or words reconfigure your thought patterns. After resetting your usual thought loops, you can rebuild your mind using a more positive thinking style.

EFT tapping technique - A great complement to these tools is the Emotional Freedom Technique (EFT), often referred to as "tapping". This practice of acupressure uses energy meridians, or pathways in the body, that have been utilized by acupuncturists for thousands of years. By tapping your fingertips on specific areas of the body, you transfer and stimulate energy to course through certain meridians. While you inject this kinetic energy into your physical body, your mental body focuses on the problem you are trying to solve. You might be processing past trauma, a bodily injury, a mental health challenge, or an addiction. Whatever the case, you can use tapping with focused intention and an element of positively charged voice affirmations. This is one of my favorite techniques for quick stress busters.

Here's how you do it: choose a finger, or multiple fingers, and then choose pressure points on your body. You can choose to tap the skin under your eye, or an area on your arm. You can tap your chest or the back of your neck. The important thing is that you're loosening your body and grounding yourself through focusing on real sensations. Some people prefer to tap with just one finger, while others use every finger and multiple pressure points. Additionally, it's suggested that you combine tapping with verbal affirmations. You can tell yourself statements such as, "I am safe," or "let the peace wash over me." You can tailor the affirmations to your specific needs and anxieties. Through combining affirmations with physical tapping, you're actually dissolving the emotional blockages and simultaneously stabilizing the mind-body connection. If you benefit from physical actions and practical solutions, tapping may be the perfect thing for you, especially during a dark night of the soul.

Grounding – Usually during the DNOS process, a person tends to become top-heavy, meaning most of the activity being in the mind or mental activity. When your mind is racing mind, grounding brings you back to the here-and-now and is very helpful in managing overwhelming feelings or anxiety. It is a great way to calm down quickly.

Grounding basically means to bring your focus to what is happening to you physically, either in your body or in your surroundings, instead of being trapped by the thoughts in your mind that are causing you to feel anxious. It helps you stay in the present moment instead of worrying about things that may happen in the future or events that have already happened.

Sit down in a comfortable chair, one where your feet reach the floor. Close your eyes and focus on your breath. Breathe in slowly for the count of three, then out slowly. Bring your mind's focus to your body.

Take a bare foot walk in the grass, imagining your excess energy is flowing down your feet into the ground. Also, the EFT technique helps; tap with your fingers just below your eyes at the bone. Repeat this for 30sec.

Integrate the process – It is easy to be top-heavy during your DNOS process. I would highly recommend to be distracted at least few times a day, so you are not in constant stress. The distractions could include going to a movie, hanging out with people whom you know, go to shopping, walk in the mall or in park, play any game you like, engage in some activity like exercise. Force yourself to do some activity at a regular interval. This will keep the mind somewhat distracted and you will have something to look forward to.

Focus on breathing – One of the most effective and probably the best technique in my opinion is paying attention to your breathing. Inhale and exhale consciously. Inhale for few seconds, hold and then exhale for few seconds. Doing this just few times a day will get you back in your physical body. This simple practice will increase your awareness and focus.

Work on suppressed emotions – All of the healing techniques in some way help you release emotions that do not serve you anymore. Here are few simple practices. Motion releases emotions, dance jump, run move to get energies moving. Scan your system for stuck energies and visualize the blockages being cleared. Also, you can write down your emotions, this is a form of outlet.

Change your environment - Psychologists believe that our environment has a massive effect on our wellbeing, both on a micro and macro level. For instance, factors such as climate, weather, and social culture play a huge role in facilitating either peace or anxiety in us. This is true on a smaller scale, too, of course. How you decorate your bedroom, the cleanliness of the street you live on, and the amount of clutter in your surroundings also has the capacity to affect your happiness and overall well-being. Therefore, if you aren't taking sufficient care of the environment around you, or if you are unhappy with your city or neighborhood, you might consider relocating.

The profound effects of our environments are never more obvious than in the workplace. Most of us spend a great majority of our time at our work locations. And the quality of the work environment can either damage or promote our mental health. If you don't agree with the work culture, for example, you may find yourself feeling excessively irritable. The same goes for dirty or sloppy work atmospheres. Plus, the social energy of a job has the power to enrich or destabilize a person. If you have found yourself in a toxic work environment, don't be afraid to change jobs. No one should have to suffer at the hands of unethical practices or demeaning work cultures. If you would benefit from working from home, or in a very specific niche environment, take the steps to make that happen. A toxic work environment can destroy one's mental health like no other.

Avoid toxic relationships - This is an intricate topic for discussion and there is no right answer. Relationships are at the core of our spiritual development. It is personal and intimate and varies for each person. Sometime we find ourself in an abusive or toxic relationship for a reason. The reason is to learn our lessons that are needed for our Soul growth. It is hard to fathom this when we are in the middle of it. I have been there, and I know this too well.

Depending upon what the Soul has to learn, the toxic relationship may have to be endured. Unfortunately, this has to do with Soul karma and there is an expiry date for Karma in such cases. This was my experience; I had to be in a relationship that did not make sense to me for a long time. Sometimes you may find yourself at the receiving end of other persons Soul lessons; in which case you do not have to put up with it. You may have to draw your boundaries and lessen/eliminate the impact to your life.

If you find yourself in situations where you feel that your energies are depleted in the presence of other person(s), you may want to consider taking action. This could be your work place, your family, your extended family or your friends. This is your life; you are entirely responsible for all things that happen to you including your environment and your relationships. I believe in you to take action.

Massage Therapy - Massage therapy works similarly to tapping. Sometimes our bodies need to relax through the help of physical sensation, especially if we're under increased stress or anxiety. Sometimes it's helpful to do more than sit with the feelings and try to analyse them away. If you're an especially physical person, massages may be a helpful means toward achieving inner peace and calm. Research suggests that massage has a plethora of healing benefits due to the fact that it releases endorphins, and endorphins are like an organic healer. But it also has a positive impact on mental health, aids in relieving body tension and chronic pain, and helps to alleviate pain brought on by aging. The Mayo Clinic acknowledges massage therapy as a hugely beneficial process. In an article written by the

Mayo Clinic press, they state, "Mayo Clinic recognizes the value of massage therapy as an aspect of wellness and has been integrating massage therapy into the hospital setting for almost 20 years."

Hypnotherapy - It's advisable to seek some form of therapy when enduring a period of depression, and the dark night of the soul is no different. Therapy is helpful for a number of reasons. It encourages you to acknowledge your emotions, release them, and receive advice and support from a nonjudgmental authority. Hypnotherapy is a specific form of therapy which involves hypnosis as a way to "reprogram" your brain. Dark nights of the soul are especially difficult for those who have childhood traumas. If you have unresolved traumas from your upbringing, the DNOS may trigger these traumas and you may benefit from more intensive therapy. If that's the case, hypnotherapy is a great option because it forces you to re-experience the difficult memory, and then create new neural pathways associated with it. That way, you can eliminate the possibility of trauma responses.

In a typical hypnotherapy session, the therapist will ask you to describe a past triggering event with vivid detail. Then, they will lead you in a sort of guided meditation. Once you're in that meditative state, through focusing on an object or the therapist's finger, your mind is ready for healing. Your subconscious is closer to the surface than usual so you have the ability to rewire it. The therapist will typically interject with new thoughts that can form the basis of a new subconscious foundation. For the majority of people, this hypnotherapy process is incredibly healing and effective.

Impact of stress on your physical body - Psychosomatic issues may arise to challenge you. These are physical symptoms that come with no medical explanation and can affect any part of your body. These are psychological issues that manifest as physical symptoms. When you have unresolved emotional issues, psychosomatic symptoms might make themselves known. This is a new way of thinking, and you have to retrain your brain to connect the experience of physical pain with an internal emotional issue that requires your attention.

The science of trauma from studying people with Post-Traumatic Stress Disorder (PTSD) reveals that pain experienced in the present time can be caused by traumas that occurred in the past. Many people with chronic pain have a history of mentally suffering from PTSD. Your nervous system is evolved to shift into survival mode when you go through traumatic events. This means that your level of cortisol, a stress hormone, increases and may remain at this sustained, heightened level until well after the event is over. In this condition, your body does not know that the trauma is over, and it has learned to respond in this way. Your blood pressure increases, your immune system weakens, and your healing ability slows. This puts your body in a constant stress state which further feeds your weakening physical health.

It's a cycle, a vicious cycle: compromised health leads to compromised health.

The good news is that you can learn to read your body's physical cues as well as your emotional pressure points. The interpretations vary, but you can start to see how things connect in yourself.

Fear manifests as weak kidneys. Worry manifests as a weak heart and brain. Grief infiltrates the lungs. Anger undermines the liver.

Wherever you feel trapped emotions in your body is also where you feel the physical ailments. Your emotional body and your pain body are closely related.

Knee pain is attached to your ego-self. Hip pain means you're afraid to move forward. Hand pain is a sign of imbalance in reaching out to others or receiving help from others. Elbow pain means you are resisting change. If your shoulders hurt, you're carrying too much and you need to lighten the load.

The physical parts of you are extended metaphors for the mental and emotional parts of you. What you feel in your body can be interpreted literally and figuratively.

If you suffer back pain, it's because you lack emotional support, or sometimes it can mean you lack financial support. You need to feel loved and secure.

Gratitude - Gratitude involves acknowledging the good things that happen, being mindful of present benefits, and recognizing that the sources of goodness are outside us. Many authors and life coaches have described gratitude as a natural feeling that surfaces from within. Most others describe being grateful or ungrateful as a choice. And as a choice, gratitude is an attitude or disposition and is more than an emotional response.

"Gratitude makes sense of our past, brings peace for today, and creates a vision for tomorrow."– Melody Beattle

Sadhguru explains that gratitude means being receptive to life.

Most people cannot receive something gracefully. Social ethics have taught us that giving is important but taking is not.

Yes, taking is not important; taking is ugly, but receiving is very important; it takes a certain amount of gratefulness and a certain amount of humility.

Just look at any aspect of your life; everything that is worthwhile you are actually receiving. For example, just think about how many people and things were involved in the clothes that you are wearing right now, from the person who planted the cottonseed to the millions of organisms that were involved in making the plant grow; from the people that prepared the cotton, from ginning to weaving to spinning to the clothing maker, agent, distributor, and seller. Even the food that you eat, just for it to get into your system—how many different lives have participated in making this happen?

If you are aware of this and if you receive gracefully, you will be overwhelmed with gratitude. Gratitude is not an attitude; it is something that flows out of you. If it is just a cultivated attitude, it is not of much significance. People have always told you that the magic words are "thank you," but gratitude is not cultivated; it happens when you are overwhelmed by something or somebody.

Suppose you were dying of hunger and somebody gave you a piece of bread, tears of gratitude would come to you. If they had given you that same piece of bread at any other moment, even if they had given you an entire loaf, it wouldn't have meant anything to you. But in that moment of hunger, you would look at the person giving you the piece of bread with enormous gratitude because you are overwhelmed by the experience. Gratitude needs not necessarily find expression in the form of eloquence; it could be just a look, a touch, a teardrop.

When you have a gratuitous mindset, you focus on the limitless opportunities available in business and life because you already appreciate what you have. When you are grateful, you choose to focus on the positive things rather than the negative things. Gratitude reduces negative thoughts and feelings. Cultivating a mindset of gratitude shifts your focus from yourself to others. Gratitude makes you feel thankful for what you have rather than always wanting more.

Gratitude creates an abundance mindset. When you focus on gratitude, what you appreciate expands and grows.

Gratitude increases your feelings of positivity and appreciation for everything in your life. Choosing gratitude and appreciation can change your life. With gratitude, your first thought is always one of positivity rather than negativity. Engaging in a regular gratitude practice can improve your mindset, self-confidence, and perspective. You feel more grateful when you focus on being thankful and feeling positive.

The very process of life is a constant phenomenon of receiving. You have nothing of your own to give; receiving is all you can do. Receive gracefully and share; that's all there is.

Forgiveness - Forgiveness is the flip side of gratitude. It involves responding positively to transgressions by offering mercy instead of vengeance. Like gratitude, it is outward-directed and intentional and recognized as a character strength. Forgiveness is often defined as an individual, voluntary internal process of letting go of feelings and thoughts of resentment, bitterness, anger, and the need for vengeance and retribution toward someone who we believe has wronged us, including ourselves.

Our capacity for forgiveness is a part of human nature that has evolved in the process of natural selection, and according to evolutionary science, it has developed in the same way as our tendency toward revenge. Science says forgiveness brings its array of health benefits, including improved relationships, decreased anxiety and stress, lower blood pressure, a lowered risk of depression, and stronger immune and heart health.

Spiritual teachings have told us that when we hold a grudge and aren't able to forgive, the person it hurts the most is the one holding the grudge.

Forgiveness does not deny pain or wrongdoing; it is a choice to let go of the person who hurt you. - You can feel forgiveness in your body. Think of times in your life when you have forgiven someone and how it made you feel. A part of you that felt heavy becomes lighter.

Forgiveness is not weakness but rather a sign of great courage and love. Think of how forgiveness can de-escalate negative thinking and situations. Think of this impact on those you are in a relationship with.

Stop being angry and forgive; you may become that anger, whatever you think about the most will grow. - Acknowledge the issue and the attached pain and anger you feel. You have to be honest with yourself if you truly want to forgive someone. - Recognize that healing takes time.

Re-conceptualize the memory. Find a new way to think about the person(s) who hurt you.

Attitude is everything - According to psychologist, Robert Puff, our mindset is a huge factor in determining how we cope with major changes and life transitions. He states,

"When big things happen, we tend to think 'I have a right to be upset.' And it's true—terrible things that happen to us will most likely make us upset—but at the same time our thoughts create our reality. If we associate experiencing something upsetting with needing to feel unhappy now, perhaps for longer, then this is going to be our reality. No matter the situation, I can almost guarantee you that someone else has gone through the same thing and they are doing absolutely fine." Puff (2021).

Puff, like most psychologists, believes that is our attitude, more than anything, which determines our happiness, or alternatively, our unhappiness. So, we are so lucky that we have knowledge about the dark night of the soul. We have examples to study, both in real life, and in the fictional stories we consume on a daily basis. We can ease our anxieties through the knowledge that darkness is essential. It leads to progress. With this mindset, we can take control of our dark night in a way that doesn't involve gripping onto old life structures. We can find peace through letting go and growing curious.

We always have the ability to reframe our thoughts. So instead of thinking, 'Wow, my is falling apart. What did I do to deserve this?' we can think, 'Wow, life as I knew it is no longer. What is my soul preparing for me, now? What do I want to do with this new freedom?' It's easier to operate from a place of positivity with this new, more optimistic outlook. Curiosity is your best friend when it comes to any major life transition. You might wonder what the caterpillar thinks as it prepares to transition in its cocoon. Is it terrified? Is it worried about the future? Or does it enter its next phase with excitement? Maybe it wonders what colors or patterns will appear on its wings? More than likely, the caterpillar doesn't have the brain capacity to ponder such questions. But even so, it's useful to think about what we gain from worrying. By now you probably know the answer...there's very little to gain from any form of fear, especially when it comes to the dark times of suffering. We can't predict how our own metamorphosis will transpire, but we can let go and give in to the mystery of the universe. We can choose to trust our souls, which is both the scariest and most exciting thing you can do as a human. If nothing else, choose to give in to the human experience. Otherwise, what's the point of even living?

* * *

We have mentioned a few helpful tools already, but let's really fill in your toolkit.

Awareness is your first tool. Be aware of your feelings and notice when you feel bogged down by the weight of all that you need to let process in your emotions. Until you become aware of your feelings, your mind will run its default program and keep cycling you through the same thoughts and anxieties. Be conscious of your thoughts and change them. Give your attention to the things you want to happen rather than focusing on what you don't want. What you put your attention on is what grows. Focus on what you do want.

Gratitude and forgiveness are also good tools to use often. Get in the habit of being grateful for what you have, and forgive the people and things in your life that could otherwise nag and distract you. Forgiveness is a gift you give yourself, for often the person you direct it to does not deserve such grace. Forgive so that you may clear your mind and heart from negativity.

Your support system is another tool for healing, including friends, family, teachers, a guru, and yourself. You are your biggest support. Take care with how you communicate with yourself internally. Pay attention to your dreams, visions, and intuitions. This is how you build a trusting relationship with yourself. Then, by extension, you will know how to strengthen your relationships with others. Be social; it helps heal the loneliness that comes with suffering. Force yourself to be social if you have to. Schedule social events. They will occupy your mind and fill some of the negative space with positive experiences.

Prayer and asking for guidance are tools. They alert your higher power that you need help—but remember that you do need to ask in order to receive.

Self-care is a tool for healing.

Try hypnotherapy, a professionally guided hypnosis that will put you into a state of deep relaxation where you can process the big emotions that need to be released.

Try meditation. If you try one style and don't like it, try another one. Try breathing meditations, moving meditations, relaxing meditations. Try everything. Guided meditations are abundant online and on various apps. Consult your doctor as needed. God helps those who help themselves, do not avoid Doctor or medication when needed.

Try a massage. The benefits are numerous. Massage reduces anxiety and depression. It eases insomnia, soothes muscles, and provides relief from arthritis and other ailments. The tactile nature of massage is healing. Human touch is healing, especially touch that presses the nerve endings in your skin to stimulate the release of your "feel good" endorphins. Massage can improve how you breath, metabolize, and circulate blood and nutrients. It stimulates your body's natural cleansing systems while improving your movement and flexibility.

In the spirit of self-care, sometimes you need to add a change of environment to your toolkit. Change is good, especially if it removes you from a toxic situation, perhaps one you were not even aware of until you have some space from it.

Your complete health and well-being come from all parts of you. Keep your body healthy with movement, nutrition, and rest. Keep your mind healthy with conscious mindfulness practices and positivity. Keep your emotions healthy by caring for yourself and allowing your emotions to release and process. Keep your relationships healthy with attention to boundaries, communication, and inter-actions that serve who you are becoming. Keep your spirit healthy by listening to and nurturing your soul's desires.

Chapter 11

Conclusion

A diamond is a piece of coal that never gave up.

My desire to live is as intense as ever, and though my heart is broken, hearts are made to be broken: that is why God sends sorrow into the world...To me, suffering seems now a sacramental thing, that makes those whom it touches holy...any materialism in life coarsens the soul. – Oscar Wilde

S uffering is a process. Healing is a process. They both begin at some point and end at another, weaving in and out of each other as they go.

There is no map for your soul's journey, but there are lighthouses along the way, signaling you to keep going. Yes, it's dark out there on an endless sea of waves that threaten to knock you down. Let these pages be a flicker of good to you as you leap into the unknown and embrace the suffering that you will one day be grateful for. Keep your eye out for the next spark of light in the dark night. Be emboldened with faith and encouraged by the same sea that will deliver you to your next phase of spiritual evolution.

When you let go of the meaning that your human mind made and voluntarily declare that it means nothing, you create a space for revitalized meaning in your soul's journey. The canvas is blank again. In this state of conceptual meaninglessness, your mind's conditioning is reset. The world looks different from this mental space. It looks like you understand nothing, and you get to experience the world again, brand new, no longer coloring it with mind-made, compulsive interpretations. You are given the chance to experience events and interactions with a sense of vitality.

Suffering is a deeply miserable process. You grow and you come through to the other side, but it is a painful and wretched experience. In your personal development along your soul's journey, suffering is meant to open you to a deeper sense of life. Its purpose is to increase your self-awareness and call attention to your thought processes and conceptual frameworks. These cognitive workings are what create your identity and the belief systems that add meaning to your life. Although it seems counterintuitive, almost like breaking a bone just so you can heal it, deep suffering is your key to spiritual growth and healing.

Some people live their whole life buying into the conventions of modern society. They live life on autopilot, allowing their ego-self to make decisions and take actions. Their life is habitual and based on their internalized conditioning from the surrounding social and cultural environment.

Other people are rudely awakened from this state of unconsciousness. Often, a personal tragedy will send these people into deep suffering where their faith wanes as they lose all sense of their former self in the process of becoming a spiritually advanced version of their highest self. Something shakes them from their daily, narrow view of life and catapults them into the darkness to be transformed.

It is not a choice, and it is not something you would choose willingly given what is known about deep suffering.

However, there is no other way sometimes. You have to come to realize that you have received a life of full conditioning from your surrounding society. You have to admit that you are who you have been shaped into by external forces. Coming to this point happens when you are mature enough to comprehend all of the components—and then there you are, a fully conditioned version of yourself. This is not a desirable state, nor is the deep suffering that ensues to separate your true essence from this false self you have been made into. It is almost always a personal crisis that kickstarts the suffering, and some believe that this kind of pressure is there to remind you that you have a unique existence that must be fully expressed if you are to thrive during this lifetime rather than simply survive.

When your soul journeys through hard times, you feel like you belong nowhere. This is your cue to turn inward and learn that you belong to yourself. Many people who enter suffering remain there for years in a state of despondent pessimism and nothingness. It is quite easy to give up, but this mentality holds you in a purgatory-like space where no growth occurs. It is a life of misery, but it is familiar and known, so many choose this option, often subconsciously, and continue to wallow in the energy of nothingness at the cost of fulfilling their soul's potential. No one blames you for this choice, especially in a modern world where there is little refuge for a weary soul. Pressures of daily life often outweigh your capacity to function, which, in turn, becomes the very threshold deep suffering uses to cross into and enter your life in the shape of a dark night of the soul.

You appear to have the choice to try to keep suffering at bay by diving into distractions, addictions, and over-analysis, but these efforts are futile and powerless to bring about a change or end the suffering. You cannot think your way through a profound struggle, nor can you drink or smoke it away. Your only real option is to become fully conscious and aware and let go of old parts of you that no longer align with who you are now. Your only choice is to get through it, and that happens with deep contemplation, meditation, and sufficient rest and relaxation.

Contemplation is necessary because you have to be honest with yourself. Once you see the falseness you have been perpetuating, you have to stop lying to yourself and own your feelings rather than berate yourself for not feeling another way. Meditation is necessary because you have to quiet the distractions and illusions that reside in your mind. You cannot reprogram your conditioned mind without first observing its workings. Then, once you exert a little conscious control over your thoughts, you begin to disrupt and reform your thought patterns. Rest and relaxation are necessary because suffering brings intense tension that builds up in your body and needs to be released. When you can be still, you can open yourself to surrender.

Some people will prove useless during this time, which is why these relationships need to fall away. Other people will make you feel like it's your fault you're suffering or you're not doing enough to try to get out of it. This is a common behavior as they don't understand the process well, either, and they have not yet embarked upon their soul's journey and are still living in collective falsity. In general, people are afraid to feel their feelings as they've likely never been taught healthy emotional processing. Instead, they use their mind to conjure up a clever escape plan to skip over feeling their feelings.

Remember, you do not need to do more during this time. What you need to do is be more. Just be. Turn off your external programming and reconnect to the fundamental experience of being alive in the current moment. Confront your shadow elements and the parts of you that you tried to bury. Go into the belly of the beast and retrieve these treasures. Allow them to be, too.

The first step in finding a shred of meaning to grasp as you are pulled through suffering is to understand the process you are experiencing and know you are not alone. Even a tiny amount of something good can bring you hope and start to ease your suffering. Follow what feels true and good. Throughout your path, you will sometimes be invigorated with sparks and clicks that awaken you more and more, and you will also endure setbacks that revert you to your previous conditioning. It's okay; you have to spend time here at this level of perception, dismantle what is false and not serving your soul's journey and awakening. Find quiet moments to practice calming the chaos of the mind, and you will begin to see the world for what it is rather than what you were told it was and what you preferred it to be. You will see there is healing through suffering.

One click review – If you believe you have gained some insight and you think others can derive some benefit as well, my request for your is to leave your valuable feedback. I appreciate your feedback so much. Thank you for your consideration. One click review link - https://www.amaz on.com/review/create-review?&asin=B0B1CMJDMJ

Free Gift to our Readers

Metamorphosis

From Darkness to Light

Click the link below or copy paste into your browser

https://mailchi.mp/d2ec904366cb/metamorphosis-freeg-ift

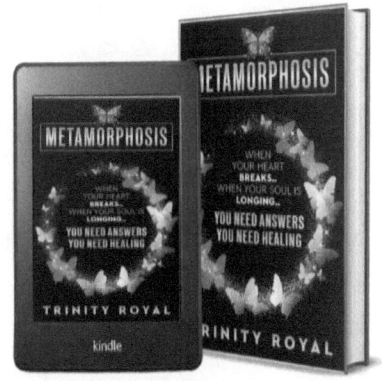

Other relevant book by the Publisher

Metamorphosis Book-2

DARK NIGHT OF THE SOUL

When your heart breaks..When your soul is longing..

You need Answers. You need Healing.

https://www.amazon.com/dp/B0B1QQCH22/

Other relevant book by the Publisher
The Super Hero Code

Superheroes aren't Born. They are made. HERE'S HOW.

https://www.amazon.com/dp/B09TWZ771R/

Chapter 12

Preview Chapter from - Metamorphosis Book-2: Dark Night of the Soul

Chapter: The Case of RED pill

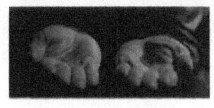

The greatest miracles aren't seen in the calm peaceful waters. They are seen in the rocky,

turbulent and frightful waters of a faith-filled life. –Kelly Balarie

Whether you know your life's purpose already or not, your destiny awaits to magnetize you to your soul's calling.

Come with me on a metaphor.

Your soul's journey begins when you take the Red Pill. Symbolically, this means that on some level of your being, you have chosen to undergo a transformative process to be of service to the world in your fullest capacity.

Take heart. You are entering into deep, dark waters that swirl and threaten to pull you under. The experience will most likely be quite different than what you anticipate. Only the rare brave souls are called onto this journey. Many of them have been preparing for many lifetimes to build up their courage. Believe that the wait is worth it and that you're ready, then dive right in.

Once you embark on this journey, you will soon find that you are traveling out of your body. It happens often and immediately after you fall asleep. The journey that your soul is on is taking you out beyond this dimension

and into heavenly realms. You will find yourself engaged in many different projects and a multitude of experiences. You will also come to know your many guides, teachers, and muses along the way who come and go as you progress through your journey. It all happens there—in the heavenly realms, where you are trained to become the best version of yourself.

There is no way to know how long this journey lasts. It can be very challenging, and depending upon your soul's blueprint for your lifetime, your training could last for years, decades, or longer. If you know and surrender to the path your soul has called you to, then enduring the process will be easier. Keep going. At each new challenge is another opportunity to develop your awareness, and as you grow in spiritual awareness, your ability to traverse the higher realms and take back information from your travels increases.

Here is how the process unfolds.

Keep in mind that the following information is subjective, and not every person goes through all of the emotions discussed here. Again, what you experience depends on what your soul's purpose is, what your destiny holds, and what you are called to do in service to humanity, the galaxy, and creation itself.

The process requires an immense amount of physical energy and perseverance. From what I've gathered in my studies, it usually begins somewhere between the ages of your mid-twenties to your late thirties. In the early stages, you will experience a lot of excitement for life anew. Your capacity to learn is exponential. You come into contact with an abundance of new information, new people, and a new awareness that starts to kick in. You feel it working *in* you, in your thought processes and ability to focus, and you feel it working *on* you as if to grow you toward your best self. You work enthusiastically, and you become a seeker of knowledge, problems, and solutions. You might even find yourself doing a lot of research, gathering your own information, exchanging ideas with friends, and asking thoughtful and thought-provoking questions of yourself and others.

You will find your higher communication channels start to open. It's the way that Source communicates with you. This is different for everyone. It can come through channels of intuition, imagination, deep listening, having visions, dreams, gut feelings, physical sensations. For me, the primary channels of communication are dreams, listening, and physical sensations in my body.

Soul Mates

As you make progress on your soul's journey, you will probably be introduced to other souls with whom you can choose to partner with for a greater purpose. Both of your souls then go through a transformation process to be compatible with each other so that together, they can make greater things happen. This kind of relationship is the literal meaning of a "match made in Heaven." Your two souls transform into harmony with each other, and your union, for however long it remains, allows you both to serve a greater purpose and service to society.

These matches are made in Heaven, though they may or may not manifest in the physical realm. It is very important that you know this, otherwise you might spend your entire lifetime in waiting mode, wondering when something will happen, and nothing might ever happen. My advice to you is to not keep waiting for Heaven to make the first move. You can take charge. Sometimes, you must take control t0 make things happen.

Give yourself permission to be this powerful. From the higher perspective that watches any two soul mates journey together, it is observable that there are times when one soul is ready for more, but the other is not. That is okay. Still, it is the source of great pain and heartache, for a lot of emotions are involved. Your heart may be pierced so badly that you wish you could force things to be different. You cannot. However, if your soul mate does show up in the physical world, then it is the sweetest thing that you can ever experience. You will know joy and ecstasy for that time of your life.

Darkness Settles In

When the Dark Night comes to transform you, every belief pattern that you hold will be challenged. The things that you hold dearly may be lost, and your dreams might crumble as you lose things that once held value. Your entire life will be laid bare. In a way, you, as you once were, will be gone.

Your mind turns hyperactive, and you become more introverted as you think about everything that comes up. You are still in your physical body, but your awareness is not—most of your mind and consciousness will be elsewhere in the world. You may be physically present, but people will intuitively sense that you are mentally absent.

Make no mistake, your heart will be pierced, you will be left longing for one drop of happiness. Your tears will seem endless. Your mental agony will be great. You might even develop migraines or other physical ailments during this time.

Very few people can relate to your suffering at this level, and no one will understand the reasons behind your depression. Any remedies you encounter will be short-lived. Your relationships may also be short-lived. Your parents, teachers, or priests will have no sufficient answers. The only other human beings who can truly understand and know your place in this process are other enlightened beings, or perhaps your spiritual guru. For that reason, you might be drawn to these people on this journey.

Many times, you will wish that this path had not chosen you. You will wish for your blissful ignorance, but in the end, this path is the choice that a higher part of you made. Like in the movie, *The Matrix*, when the Oracle says to Neo, "You have already made the choice." Your journey will help you understand why so that you can make the best of it. The only thing you have in the Dark Night of the Soul is your faith and trust in a higher power and yourself.

A fire burns deep in your soul, a flame that does not extinguish even during the most difficult circumstances. This is your faith, and it is the only thing that will lead you through your soul's suffering. Yes, your faith will flicker. Yes, you will lose it time and again, but you will also recover it every time. This happens cyclically as you transform.

You will go through multiple phases of "ego deaths" that shed your old ways of being, too. Your heart will be pierced multiple times.

....snip....

If you like this preview from one chapter, you will love the **Metamorphosis Book-2: Dark Night of the Soul** — https://www.amazon.com/dp/B0B1QQCH22/

Glossary

Conscious Mind: The part of the mind that is aware of governing thoughts and actions.

Depression: A mood disorder that triggers prolonged sadness and apathy.

Ego: A person's sense of self-importance; the part of the mind that construct's identity and is in charge of reality testing.

Emotional Freedom Technique (EFT): Also called 'tapping', this is a form of therapy for potent stress relief.

Energy Healing: A type of holistic therapy that uses the body's energy circuits to facilitate healing by unblocking energy tracks identifying problems before they manifest as pain or illness.

External Manifestation: Events and occurrences that enter a person's reality from an outside source.

Higher Power: Refers to a divine, supreme being or other conception of God.

Internal Manifestation: Events and occurrences that enter a person's reality and stem from inside of them.

Karma: The sum of all actions in this and previous lifetimes that decide a person's destiny or fate in a future lifetime.

Manifestation: Refers to strategies that bring about a person's intended goal and are based on the Law of Attraction and positive thinking that expects the universe to intercede.

Mantra: A sound, word, or phrase that is repeated in meditation.

Meditation: A mind and body practice to increase calmness, relaxation, psychological balance, and overall well-being.

Metamorphosis: The transformation process that matures a being in distinct, unique stages.

Positive Disintegration: A theory of personality development where anxiety and tension are necessary for personal growth.

Post-Traumatic Stress Disorder (PTSD): A mental health disorder that stems from a traumatic event and is characterized by distress, anxiety, flashbacks, and intrusive thoughts.

Psychosomatic: Refers to symptoms that are caused by the interaction between the body and the mind; a physical response to a mental health issue.

Sound Healing: A form of therapy that uses music and frequencies to balance a person's energy in the body and mind.

Source: The non-physical, conscious energy of creation that can be attracted and aligned to.

Spiritual Awakening: The experience of collapsing your sense of separation from oneness that usually begins with dissolving the ego.

Spiritual Evolution: The idea that the spirit evolves from a simple form that is ruled by nature to a higher form that is ruled by divinity.

Subconscious Mind: The part of the mind not presently in focused awareness.

Synchronicity: When events that have no causal connection occur simultaneously and appear significantly related.

Trauma: A deeply disturbing, stressful experience that may include physical injury or emotional shock and can lead to long-term neurosis.

Unconscious Mind: The deep recesses of a person's memories and past.

Universe: All of space and time, and all of matter and energy.

References

7 omens that herald the dark night of the soul. (2020, October 2). LonerWolf. https://lonerwolf.com/the-dark -night-of-the-soul/

12 things not to do if you're suffering from depression. (n.d.). Intrepid Mental Health. https://www.intrepidmentalhealth.com/blog/1 2-things-not-to-do-if-youre-suffering-from-depression

18 signs you're experiencing a dark night of the soul, otherwise known as an existential crisis. (2017, February 9). Thought Catalog. https://thoughtcatalog.com/brianna-wiest/2017/02/18- signs-youre-going-through-whats-known-as-a-dark-night -of-the-soul/

A dark night of the soul and the discovery of meaning. (n.d.). Kosmos Journal. https://www.kosmosjournal.org/article/a-dark-nigh t-of-the-soul-and-the-discovery-of-meaning/

A flicker of faith. (2016, January 15). Ram Dass. https ://www.ramdass.org/flicker-of-faith/

Abraham Lincoln Quotes. (n.d.). Quote Fancy. https:// quotefancy.com/abraham-lincoln-quotes

Blaize, A. (2020, June 10). The Dark Night of the Soul. Law of Connections. https://medium.com/law-of-conn ections/the-dark-night-of-the-soul-c33a0c7ee023

Boomer, S. (2020). What is your soul's journey (and where is your final destination?). Awake and Align. http s://awakeandalign.com/souls-journey/

Brown, M. (n.d.). [Silhouette of window vane]. Pexels. https://www.pexels.com/photo/silhouette-of-wind-vane-552600/

Davis, L. (2016, July 9). *How your emotions are causing you physical pain, science explains.* The Minds Journal. https://themindsjournal.com/physical-pain-correlat es-emotional-pain/

Depression or Dark Night of the Soul? (2021, September 28). Soul Shepherding. https://www.soulshepherdin g.org/depression-or-dark-night-of-the-soul/

Eckhart, M., & Stryz, J. (2003). The Wisdom of Meister Eckhart. New Grail.

Eckhart on the Dark Night of the Soul. (2018, April 2). Eckhart Tolle | Official Site - Spiritual Teachings and Tools for Personal Growth and Happiness. https://eckharttoll e.com/eckhart-on-the-dark-night-of-the-soul/

Frontline. (n.d.). *The Long Walk of Nelson Mandela* [Video]. https://www.pbs.org/wgbh/pages/frontline/sh ows/mandela/interviews/alexander.html

Gibran, K. (2012). Broken Wings. Bottom Of The Hill Publishing.

Googins, D. (n.d.). On the Other Side of Suffering is Greatness. YouTube. https://www.youtube.com/watch?v=B9YhjPP3b2s

Joyful confidence in God: the dark night of the soul. (n.d.). Faith Gateway. https://www.faithgateway.com/joyful-confidence-god-dark-night-soul/#.YjKYTHrMLFg

Meyer, J. (2018). Battlefield of the Mind Study Guide: Winning the Battle in your Mind. Faith Words.

May, G. G. (n.d.). The Dark Night of the Soul. Spirituality & Practice. https://www.spiritualityandpractice.com/book-reviews/view/8234/the-dark-night-of-the-soul

Mcnutt III, S. (2018). Care Package : A Path to Deep Healing. Success Is A Choice.

Myss, C. M. (2004). Anatomy of the Spirit, and Why People Don't Heal and How They Can. Gramercy Books.

Nelson, B. (2019). The Emotion Code : How to Release Your Trapped Emotions for Abundant Health, Love, and Happiness. St. Martin's Essentials.

Nietzsche, F.W. & Common, T. (2021). Thus Spake Zarathustra. Binker North.

Norton, B. (n.d.). Why suffering is required for spiritual growth (Healing Depression, Anxiety, and Trauma

[Video]. YouTube. https://www.youtube.com/watch?v =q-wabqwMc-A

Onkka, L. (n.d.). Heal yourself and end suffering with [Video]. YouTube. https://www.youtube.com/watch?v =Pd5w5iEEkCA

Press, J. (2022, February 26). The dark night of the soul: understanding amidst the absence of meaning. Medium. https://theapeiron.co.uk/the-dark-night-of-the-soul-und erstanding-amidst-the-absence-of-meaning-3494cb193bc 2

Project Life Mastery. (n.d.). How to free yourself from emotional pain & suffering [Video]. YouTube. https://w ww.youtube.com/watch?v=lzy64MccvoQ

Richo, D. (1991). How to Be an Adult : A Handbook on Psychological and Spiritual Integration. Paulist Press.

Ritt, M. J., Hill, N., Cypert, S. A., & Sartwell, M. (2007). Napoleon Hill's Positive Action Plan: 365 Meditations for Making Each Day a Success. Plume.

Sadhguru. (n.d.). How do you eliminate suffering when suffering is all that you have left? [Video]. YouTube. https://www.youtube.com/watch?v=t-z_3oBnMdI

Salmansohn, K. (2001). How to Be Happy, Dammit : A Cynic's Guide to Spiritual Happiness. Celestial Arts.

TEDx Talks. (2015). Healing illness with the subconscious mind | Danna Pycher [Video]. YouTube. https://www.youtube.com/watch?v=erpPQDSWD0k

Tolle, E. (n.d.). Simple Recipe for Overcoming Suffering [Video]. YouTube. https://www.youtube.com/watch?v=xANjrN3rVvE

Understanding the dark night of the senses & the soul. (n.d.). The Young Catholic Woman. https://www.theyoungcatholicwoman.com/archivescollection/understanding-the-dark-night-of-the-senses-amp-the-soul

What was Paul's thorn in the flesh? (2 Corinthians 12). (2021, December 29). Crossway. https://www.crossway.org/articles/what-was-pauls-thorn-in-the-flesh-2-corinthians-12/

Whyte, D. (2011). The House of Belonging: Poems. Many Rivers Press.

Wilde, O., & Holland, M. (2007). Oscar Wilde: A Life In Letters. Carroll & Graf.

Words, C. (2014, April 17). "Sweet Darkness" by David Whyte. Words for the Year. https://wordsfortheyear.com/2014/04/17/sweet-darkness-by-david-whyte/

Zebian, N. (2018). The Nectar of Pain. Andrews Mcmeel Publishing.

Image References

Araja, E. (n.d.). [Monochrome photo of person standing on hallway]. Pexels. https://www.pexels.com/photo/monochrome-photo-of-person-standing-on-hallway-3343253/

Ferlin, J. (n.d.). [Human hand photo]. Pexels. https://www.pexels.com/photo/left-human-hand-photo-3025562/

Grabowska, K. (n.d.). [White and black gift box]. Pexels. https://www.pexels.com/photo/white-and-black-gift-box-5632349/

Pixabay. (n.d.-a). [Clear glass with red sand grainer]. Pexels. https://www.pexels.com/photo/clear-glass-with-red-sand-grainer-39396/

Pixabay. (n.d.-b). [Yellow and black butterflies cocoon]. Pexels. https://www.pexels.com/photo/yellow-and-black-butterflies-cocoon-39862/

Ravsanjani Gusma, N. A. (n.d.). White sparklings. Pexels. https://www.pexels.com/photo/white-sparklings-2422583/

Sedaghat, F. (n.d.). [Mysterious shadow behind dark backdrop]. Pexels. https://www.pexels.com/photo/mysterious-shadow-behind-dark-backdrop-3809379/

Shaffer, E. (n.d.). [Diamond on a white surface]. Pexels. https://www.pexels.com/photo/diamond-on-white-surface-4997547/

Ulsh, A. (n.d.). [Blue water]. Pexels. https://www.pexels.com/photo/blue-water-2860705/